VERNON WATKINS and the SPRING OF VISION

VERNON WATKINS
and the
SPRING of VISION

DORA POLK

Christopher Davies
Swansea

Published in 1977 by
Christopher Davies (Publishers) Ltd
4/5 Thomas Row
Swansea SA1 1NJ

*Printed in Wales by
Salesbury Press Ltd
Swansea*

ISBN 0 7154 0349 4

Published with the support of the Welsh Arts Council

TABLE OF CONTENTS

ACKNOWLEDGEMENTS

I am grateful to Mrs. Gwen Watkins, for permission to quote from the poems of Vernon Watkins. I also wish to express my appreciation to California State University at Long Beach for a Sabbatical Leave and a grant from the Foundation which make possible the completion of this book.

D.P.

INTRODUCTION

S. L. Bethell, lecturer in English during my undergraduate days at University College, Cardiff, first made me aware of the work of Vernon Watkins. That was in the early forties, shortly after Watkins's "Ballad of the Mari Lwyd" was published by Faber on the recommendation of T. S. Eliot. Mr. Bethell had a profound influence on my life, though not in the sense that I would blindly accept his judgements—a posture he would have deplored in any case. He was in the vanguard of the New Criticism, evolving a critical method to put the student into personal possession of a literary work so that he could make an independent assessment of its merits. But Mr. Bethell's mention of Watkins at least had the force of alerting me to the emergence of a new Welsh voice worthy of attention, if I could ever find the time to steep myself in the poetry, as the Bethell method required.

Formal studies, then job responsibilities and the ordinary business of living permitted me only a desultory interest in Watkins over the next couple of decades. Much of Watkins's work was arcane and opaque to me, as, apparently, it was to many other readers—to judge by the poverty of commentary during that period. But more and more that "gut reaction," which I came increasingly to trust in myself, told me that I must one day find time to come to grips with the canon for my soul's sake.

In the sixties, I had a chance to return to a more concentrated study of literature, particularly to the mystic and hermetic traditions in Celtic literature, which had always fascinated me. Under Professor Hazard Adams at the University of California at Irvine, I became deeply interested in the work of Yeats—a natural pathway back to Watkins, with whose growing corpus I became increasingly engaged. My hold upon Watkins's work was significantly aided by the insights provided by Kathleen Raine's milestone essay in the Spring, 1964, issue of *The Anglo-Welsh Review*.

The fact that I eventually diverged somewhat from Ms. Raine's approach in no way invalidates the access she provided me to Watkins's work. Without her help I might never have become the beneficiary of Watkins's vision, which, after all, is what the study of poetry is all about. Literary criticism does not involve the rejection of earlier monographs in favour of later ones. Rather, individual papers, essays and reviews are contributions to a continuing, burgeoning discussion, whose contours are preserved by acknowledgement as each new commentator cites works on which his own observations depend — concurring, demurring, adding, modifying, as the case may be. The new student may then see for himself the flux of debate thus far, and thereby come to understand not just the work at issue, but the process by which earnest and persistent readers make difficult works yield up their mysteries.

This view of the cumulative nature of literary criticism also provides the rationale for the belated publication in book form of this study—for which I am most grateful to the publishers. Begun in 1967 — the year Watkins came to the West Coast only to meet his untimely death—and completed in 1970, it has to date been circulated only in manuscript to a handful of people interested in the work of Watkins.

Because so little critical attention had been paid to Watkins's work at the time this study was begun—as revealed by Jane McCormick's valuable bibliography in the Spring, 1968, issue of *West Coast Review*—I had to win access to Watkins's work by the fumbling methods of the explorer who lacks maps or accounts to help him, and must rely principally on his own ingenuity and the tools he carries on his back. And, to continue the metaphor, my findings are recorded rather in the manner of a pioneer's log—a tentative account of the personal process of discovery of Watkins's vision. The delay in publication of these findings in book form naturally raised the question of whether they should be reshaped into a more formal and conventional presentation. Also raised was the question of whether the work ought to be "corrected" or "updated" in the light of intervening research set forth in various essays and books which have appeared since the dissertation was first submitted. But since the main purpose of its publication is to fill in the gaps in the emerging body of Watkins criticism to provide a continuous record, it seemed important to stick as close to the original text as possible—especially as my views remain substantially the same.

I am lucky enough to teach poetry to undergraduates, and seize every occasion to include something by Watkins on lists of modern and contemporary work. I cannot speak for the majority of students, but there are always one or two who declare their perspective changed by even a glimpse of Watkins's vision. Moreover, I know that the more often I read a poem by Watkins, the more profoundly it speaks to me—which must be as valid a test as the bristling-hair theory of Housman and Graves for discerning true poetry.

CHAPTER I

BACKGROUND, RATIONALE, AND
CRITICAL METHOD

During his lifetime, Vernon Watkins published many hundreds of poems, the most important of which have been collected in the volumes entitled *Ballad of the Mari Lwyd and Other Poems* (1941), *The Lamp and the Veil* (1945), *The Lady with the Unicorn* (1948), *The Death Bell* (1954), *Cypress and Acacia* (1959), *Affinities* (1962), and, posthumously, *Fidelities* (1968).[1] Despite this substantial corpus produced over several decades, critical commentary on his work (even including reviews) had remained small until a few years before his death, when such essays as Kathleen Raine's "Vernon Watkins: Poet of Tradition"[2] began to give the poet his due. Now that the canon appears to have been completed with the publication of *Uncollected Poems* (London, 1969), there will undoubtedly be a further quickening of interest in Watkins's work. Too long distinguished mainly for his relationship to Dylan Thomas, Watkins is at last being appreciated as a poet of considerable dimension in his own right, a view that this work was undertaken to support.

Watkins was born on June 27, 1906, in Maesteg, South Wales, a typically depressing colliery town in the Llynfi Valley of Glamorganshire, just north of Bridgend. In 1918, Watkins

---

1 All published by Faber and Faber Limited, London. Parenthetical page references to Watkins's poems are in these editions.
2 *The Anglo-Welsh Review*, XIV, No. 33 (1964), 20-38; reprinted in *Defending Ancient Springs* (London, 1967), pp. 17-34. Parenthetical page references are to the latter.

moved with his parents to the Gower Peninsula, an area pro-
jecting eighteen or so miles into the Bristol Channel between
Swansea Bay and the Burry Inlet of Carmarthen Bay, and contrasting vividly with the bleakness of the mining region from
which he came. On the Gower's rugged and beautiful coastline,
whose scenery provided much of the concrete imagery in
Watkins's poetry, the poet spent the rest of his life—though
there were important interludes away for such purposes as
attendance at school and college, residence in Cardiff at his first
job, and service in the Royal Air Force from 1941 to 1946
during World War II. On Pennard Cliffs, Gower, he and his
wife Gwen, whom he married in 1944, reared their family of
four sons and a daughter. And on Gower, in the churchyard of
his Parish Church at Pennard, rest his remains. He died of a
heart attack in October 1967 shortly after arrival in Seattle,
Washington, for a year's sojourn as visiting Professor of
English at the University of Washington.

As the son of middle-class parents, Watkins completed his
preparatory education at Repton, the famous public school in
Derbyshire, which Watkins celebrates in "Revisited Waters"
(*Affinities,* p. 89), written for the quater-centenary of the
school in 1957. He went up to Magdalene College, Cambridge,
to read modern languages, but remained there only a year,
deciding, instead, in 1925, to take up, after his father's example,
the career of banking. But, as he was fond of telling against himself, whereas his father, William Watkins, had the distinction of
being one of the youngest bank managers in Lloyd's history, he,
Vernon Watkins, must surely have been the bank's oldest clerk,
a position he still held at his retirement from the St. Helen's
Road Branch of Lloyd's in Swansea in 1966 after more than
forty years of service. By all accounts an efficient and responsible employee, incredibly quick with figures and fond of
mathematics, he was nonetheless without material ambitions,
eschewing promotion in order to conserve his resources for
writing poetry.[3] He apparently regarded his banking job solely

3 "The Poet Who was A-1 at Lloyds," Swansea *Evening Post,* October 10,
1967, p. 4.

as the means to supply the bread-and-butter needs of himself and his family while he pursued his true vocation. Believing poetry was "not of the market place,"[4] never expecting to gain recognition in his lifetime, much less to support himself, by his writing, he successfully managed to meet the competing demands of his life—responsibility to his family, responsibility to his art—by the simple expedient of remaining content with a routine job.

The curtailment of Watkins's university career had by no means meant the curtailment of his education. Quite the contrary, he had freed himself to determine his own intellectual growth according to his creative needs. He was fortunate to find stimulation and encouragement through association with the talented Swansea group made legendary more by the renown of Dylan Thomas than by that of any other of its perhaps equally brilliant members, among whom were Daniel Jones, the composer, Alfred Janes, the artist, John Ormond, who made a celebrated film of Watkins, as well as Watkins himself. The collection of letters from Dylan Thomas to Watkins, published in 1956 as *Letters to Vernon Watkins,* bears testimony to the reciprocally nourishing friendship between the two men lasting until Thomas's death in 1953.

Watkins nurtured his intellect by a wide variety of reading in literature and traditional lore. Dr. Daniel Jones has spoken of the depth and breadth of Watkins's knowledge, which Watkins's modesty had always contrived to conceal: "He hid the fact that he was very well read, not only in English literature but also in many other languages. . . . He had the knowledge of an academic and he was capable of giving the kind of lecture Dylan would have found impossible."[5] Pursuing his love for European languages which his year at Cambridge had re-inforced, Watkins translated throughout his life the work of German, French and Italian poets, being especially devoted to Heine and Hölderlin, and to various French *sym-*

---

4 "Memorial Service Tributes to Poet Vernon Watkins," Swansea *Evening Post,* March 11, 1968, p. 2.
5 "Tributes to the Poet," Swansea *Evening Post,* October 9, 1967, p. 3.

bolistes. After the Hungarian revolution of 1956, he even turned his hand to the translation of Hungarian poetry at the request of a group of refugees.

Even if we had no other testimony than Watkins's own poetry, we could infer his learning from the complex fabric of myth and symbol out of which his work is woven. As Kathleen Raine has put it, Watkins "chose tradition (vital memory) as against education, and inspiration as against the new positivist spirit of the age" (p. 18). He was deeply devoted to the English mystics such as Rolle and Julian of Norwich, and read extensively and intensively in the poets of the religious and hermetic tradition. Like Yeats, whom he admired tremendously, believing him "the greatest poet of this century,"[6] Watkins was familiar with the Neo-Platonists, as citations and quotations from Plotinus's *Enneads* in his notebook suggest.[7] Like Yeats he was engaged by the folk tradition of his country, which he came at by osmosis and by reading. While modestly declining any more than a superficial comparison, Watkins points out that just as Yeats "used Irish legends in his early work,"[8] so he used the Welsh permutations of Celtic folklore in his first poems, as in the "Ballad of the Mari Lwyd." By rejecting formal education in favour of self-instruction and participation in this occult, mystical, mythic and bardic tradition, Kathleen Raine believes that Watkins gave himself a great advantage "over poets whose sources are solely literary" (p. 21), and won himself a permanent place among the metaphysical poets.

Despite the paucity of critical comment on his work, Watkins's private route to wisdom and accomplishment did not go unacknowledged. In 1951, he was made a Fellow of the Royal Society of Literature. In 1953, he was awarded the Levinson Prize from *Poetry* (Chicago), and in March, 1954, his

---

6 See Ron Berry, "Vernon Watkins' 43rd Year of Poetry Making," *Swansea Voice*, April 15, 1960, p. 4.

7 The notebooks were kindly made available to me by Mrs. Gwen Watkins in the summer of 1968.

8 Ron Berry, "Vernon Watkins' 43rd Year of Poetry Making."

volume *The Death Bell* was the first choice of the Poetry Book
Society. In 1957, he earned the Guinness Poetry Award for
"The Tributary Seasons," and in 1967 received an honorary
D.Litt. from the University of Wales, becoming, in the same
year, the first holder of the Calouste Gulbenkian Fellowship of
Poetry at University College, Swansea. In addition to these
tokens of public esteem, he was held in high regard by his fellow
poets. Dylan Thomas (characteristically excepting only himself) called Watkins the finest poet writing in the nineteen
thirties, a tribute Marianne Moore updated several decades
later. T. S. Eliot discerned Watkins's powers from the first, with
his recommendation of the "Ballad of the Mari Lwyd."

Ironically, Watkins was himself largely responsible for the
critical reticence about his work. Those who valued his work
knew that his modest, retiring nature required privacy in which
to produce it, and were concerned to help provide that privacy.
Then, too, Watkins's own reluctance to make judgements
about the work of living authors put those who admired him
into a dilemma. To make public their esteem would violate that
deep conviction of the poet, a breach they presumably could
not bring themselves to commit, especially after Watkins's reticence about Dylan Thomas even after Thomas's death.

Even more influential in stopping critical comment and thus
wider acclaim was Watkins's belief in the intransigence of the
poetic word. He held that a poem could not be equated or
"translated" or converted in any way; it was itself and no other.
So firmly did he hold this view that, out of distrust of dramatic
additives, he even discouraged interpretive performances of his
work, believing that "the words should speak for themselves."[10]

Explication appears to have been associated in Watkins's

9 For a more complete listing of Watkins's awards, see Jane McCormick,
   "Vernon Watkins: A Bibliography," *West Coast Review*, IV, No. 1 (1968),
   42-48.
10 See the comments of Elizabeth M. Jones in "Four Tributes", *The Anglo-
   Welsh Review*, XVII, No. 39 (1968), 11, and Dr. Daniel Jones in "Tributes
   to the Poet."

mind with the cold hand of science and positivism which "murders to dissect." In the poem "Exegesis" the poet contends that the many voices of literary critics, as of exegetes of the Bible over the centuries, cannot replace the single voice of the poet; they can only falsify him, and unless they restrain themselves, "the truth will lie."

> So many voices
> Instead of one.
> Light, that is the driving force
> Of song alone:
> Give me this or darkness,
> The man or his bone.
>
> None shall replace him,
> Only falsify
> Light broken into colours,
> The altered sky.
> Hold back the bridle,
> Or the truth will lie.
>
> (*Fidelities*, p. 51)

It follows from this that the introductory sentence to the poem above is a violation of its spirit and a distortion of its truth.

Apparently it was not fear of the ravages and outrages of the critics that made Watkins averse to explication so much as the firm belief that he had said what he had to say in the most lucid way possible, as Elizabeth M. Jones's account of the 1949 production of the "Ballad of the Mari Lwyd" reveals:

> We discussed difficulties sometimes over lunch. . . . If I asked him to elucidate any passage of which the meaning had not seemed clear to us at rehearsal the evening before, he always listened with grave interest and politeness, but I never felt he had the slightest idea of where any difficulty could lie. Having laboured to convey his meaning in the most lucid and vivid words at his command, he felt, quite rightly, that saying the same thing in some other way was unlikely to clarify things for anyone. I remember telling him that one player was having difficulty with a particular line, and he only said, "Yes, yes, it seems very clear really doesn't it?"[11]

He did come to recognize, however, that for the ordinary reader there were difficulties inherent in his very vision which

11 "Four Tributes," p. 11.

mere clarity of expression could not dispel. He put this down to the fact that artists "are ahead of their time," arguing:

> Their heightened sensitivity already experiences what appears only gradually to their fellow men. They present what is already known, but with an enhanced judgment; and they reveal what is unfamiliar, new aspects of form which are brought into the realm of common understanding. The works of a great master represent the need and the gift in their highest and most intense operation. Paradoxically such works may have been scarcely recognized in the lifetime of the artist. A town's richest treasure may be the works of a man who had this need and this gift, and who died penniless. Artists are the antennae of the race, and in the past it usually took a generation, or more than one, to catch up with their genius. In poetry, genuine recognition often comes later still, and a century may pass before the true need of the poet is reflected in his audience.[12]

Taken together, these views suggest Watkins's faith in the ultimate emergence of an audience with a background of learning and experience at least as sophisticated and unusual as his own, an audience capable of grasping each poem completely, without the aid of explicators, exegetes, or literary critics, an audience forearmed with the vast fund of knowledge and experience obviating recourse to the distorting aid of gloss and footnote.

At the beginning of the seventeenth century, this might have been a reasonable expectation. A certain cultural homogeneity and a relatively compact body of knowledge provided a common context out of which the poet wrote and the reader read. This is no longer the case. As Kathleen Raine points out, contemporary society "as a whole has lost that unity of culture which belonged to Christendom (which included and perpetuated the earlier Classical tradition)," with the result that symbolic discourse is reduced to "a private, lyrical language" (pp. 118-119). Beliefs and backgrounds are infinitely various in contemporary society, and a man with a composite or encyclopedic background—especially coupled with the great awareness and sensitivity that aesthetic appreciation demands—is bound to become increasingly rare.

12 "The Need of the Artist," *The Listener,* November 8, 1962, p. 756.

Watkins's expectation is all the more forlorn when we consider that the background of Celtic myth, folklore and hermetic symbolism out of which he wrote is now quite alien to large numbers of English-speaking people. Even the Christian context, necessary to an appreciation of Watkins's work, is no longer commonplace.

The "ideal audience" that Watkins's statements appear to assume has been more hypothetical than real since at least the Romantic Reaction. Looking back on the way earlier poets came to be recognized, we find that audiences seldom came ready-made, even when potential readers were adequately equipped to handle a given canon. We find a process something like this: one or two people are touched by a poem or parts of poems; they express their appreciation, inspiring others to read. Further readers share their experiences, throwing light on obscurities, and the work is made available to an even wider audience. In the case of Blake, the observations of Gilchrist, followed by those of Swinburne and Rossetti, led to the more painstaking elucidations of the *Memoir and Interpretation* of Ellis and Yeats, which, in turn, were followed by a swiftly accelerating flow of exegesis and commentary throughout the twentieth century. It is this snowballing phenomenon, a pooling of information and interpretation, and a rebuttal of misinformation and misinterpretation, which creates an informed clerisy in an age when the reader stands little chance of becoming the modern equivalent of a cultivated Renaissance man. The poet might prefer no audience at all to one using a "reconstituted" or "prefabricated" background. But the reader has needs and demands, too; he is not likely to defer to the wishes of the poet if he senses, or hears tell, that the poetry may be worth reading. He will try to seize control of the poem the best way he can. His experience of the work of art may not be as deep, rich and immediate as that of the widely educated and experienced man, or of the painstaking reader who has carefully built for himself such a background as the poems demand. But it will be better than no experience at all.

My own efforts to gain possession of Watkins's poems involved a piecemeal acquisition of background, and a fumbling quest for "keys" that might let me in to his particular vision. What I tried to create for myself was an ambience in which the poems could come alive for me. Ideally, this field or ambience should approximate the total "creative ground" out of which a given poem grew. What are recorded here, however, are mere fragments of the whole recovered to date. Ultimately it is to be hoped that enough information and interpretation will be generated and pooled by critics everywhere to provide the inexperienced reader with a readily assimilable "context" with which to brief himself to advantage before proceeding to his own reading of the poems.

It might be argued that the compiling of such a ground or context might be faster accomplished by a wide-spectrum study of the poet's cultural milieu, and a reconstruction through biographical research of the poet's views and interests. These studies will undoubtedly be undertaken in due course, and will undoubtedly cast important illumination. But my own preference is for an approach rooted in the poems themselves. My concern is to work empiricically outwards from the poems individually, seeking answers to specific doubts, and clarification of particular obscurities, as they are met, moving thence to comparisons and contrasts among the poems, which process, in turn, leads to the discovery of recurrent themes and preoccupations throughout the canon. Since a good many of these answers came from recovery of myth, symbol and folklore, much of this commentary is essentially a gloss.

Any commentary, of course, has to be read with continuous reference to the poems themselves. I have tried to minimise inconvenience by liberal quotation.

It should be emphasized, too, that what is offered as "keys" is whatever material happened to help me grasp the poem. No claim is made that the poet himself ever saw the material cited, quoted, or summarized. Indeed, many works to which I refer were not in existence at the time the poem under consideration was written. For example, Robert Graves's *The White Goddess,* to which I have referred extensively in order to provide a context for the "Ballad of the Mari Lwyd," was written in 1944 and published in 1946, whereas the Ballad had its genesis

19

in 1938, and was published in 1941. All we may assume is that the poet possessed information comparable to that here presented, he having gained it from first-hand experience and oral accounts, or from the reading of original manuscripts and texts, other primary sources, and older secondary sources. Identification of precise sources of the poet's knowledge is something for future study.

Needless to say, no claim is made for the factual "truth" of the assertions offered as background, nor should any inferences be drawn that the poet actually "believed in" any myth or legend forming the raw material out of which a given poem was created. I have elected to limit my responsibility only to suggesting that knowledge of the legend or myth cited seems important to an adequate experience of the poem, which is another way of saying I am to be held accountable only for my deductions that such and such a legend or myth seems to have been part of the poetic stock out of which the poem was created. What this comes down to is the hypothetical reconstruction of some of the poet's "ground" achieved by coming to grips with the poems which emerged from that "ground." These uncorroborated findings are conveyed to the reader in the conviction that they will improve his grasp, or deepen his experience, of the poem.

In this preamble for a continuing study, I have confined myself principally to a quest for the "keys"—or to use the other metaphor, the ambience—to the "Ballad of the Mari Lwyd," both because this was one of Watkins's first poems—it gave its name to his first volume—and because a solid grasp of this poem makes clearer a considerable number of other poems in the canon, several of which will be discussed at relevant points. As Kathleen Raine puts it: "This poem seems an initiation which the poet has received from the ancestors, which has continued to fertilize all his future work" (p. 25), an assertion which, in effect, constitutes the working thesis of this study.

CHAPTER II

THE RELATIONSHIP OF THE "BALLAD OF THE MARI LWYD" TO THE WELSH CUSTOM OF THE MARI LWYD

Although Watkins repeatedly opposed "interpretation" or "exposition" of his work, he apparently recognized the reader's need for specialized information extrinsic to his "Ballad of the Mari Lwyd," for he supplies an after-note. Perhaps he did this at the suggestion of the publisher; a pencilled note on the typescript in the British Museum reads: "Does the Ballad need some kind of a note or clue?"

The note reads in part as follows:

> Mari Lwyd—the Grey Mari, the Grey Mare—was, by tradition in Wales, carried from house to house on the last night of the year. It was a horse's skull. Sometimes it was supplanted by a copy, a white or grey horse's head modelled in wood, painted and hung with ribbons, but in all examples of the true tradition the skull itself was used. The skull had been chosen and buried when the horse died, and the burial-place marked, so that it could be exhumed for the ceremony. After it, the skull was kept, and used again on the next thirty-first of December, and so on year after year.

> The carriers were usually a party of singers, wits and impromptu poets, who, on the pretext of blessing, boasted of the sanctity of what they carried, tried to gain entrance to a house for the sake of obtaining food and drink. The method they used was to challenge those within to a rhyming contest. The inmates could keep them out so long as they were not in want of a rhyme, but when they failed to reply to the challenger the right of entry was gained. The singers would then bring their horse's head in, lay it on the table, and eat and drink with the losers of the contest. (pp. 89-90)

In his article entitled "New Year 1965," Watkins pinpoints the experience out of which his poem "began to take shape":

21

> I was already living on this cliff [Pennard Cliffs, his home on the
> Gower Coast outside Swansea] before the war, and I remember
> coming home very late on the last night of the year 1938. It was
> just before midnight, and I caught the sound of a broadcast of the
> Mari Lwyd ceremony which was coming from my father's old
> home at Taff's Well: that ceremony traditional in Wales, in which
> a horse's skull was carried from house to house on the last night of
> the year by a party of singers, wits, and impromptu poets, usually
> the worse for drink, who challenged the inmates to a rhyming
> contest, and, if they won, claimed entry and the right to food and
> ale.[1]

The salient features of the custom as Watkins knew it are
woven into his Ballad. As in the folk rite described in the note
and the article, the outsiders in the poem are led by the Mari,
"Horse of Frost, Star-Horse, and White Horse of the Sea," "a
white horse frozen blind," a "mounted, murderous thing," a
braying mare that "through the night they carry." The line "a
horse's head in the frost" serves as the Ballad's major refrain.

Watkins also used the notion of the rhyming contest as the
basic structure of his poem, which unfolds as a dramatic exchange between those without and those within. Like the petitioners in the time-honoured custom, the outsiders of the poem
demand:

> Give us rhyme for rhyme through the wood of the door
> Then open the door if you fail. (p. 74)

And:

> Oh rhyme with us now through the keyhole's slit
> And open the door if you fail. (p. 75)

The outsiders appeal in the traditional way for pity:

> O pity us, brothers, through snow and rain
> We are come from Harlech's waves. (p. 74)

They make the usual extravagant promises for the price of a
drink:

> We have come with blessing to heal your sight
> If first you will cool our tongue. (p. 84)

1 *The Listener,* January 7, 1965, pp. 22-23.

But the insiders spurn their pleas, and scoff at their claims, calling them lies:

> When the big stars stare and the small stars wink
> You cry it's the break of day.
>
> Out of our sight; you are blind with drink:
> Ride your Mari away. (p. 84)

In the middle of the Ballad, the impromptu rhyming contest is captured most precisely by an exchange of quatrains, charge and countercharge, expostulation and reply, the inmates never wanting for a retort.

But the petitioners do not give up easily. They try every ruse they know to gain entry at the locked door to reach the fire inside and partake of such local delicacies and refreshments as the "Felinfoel beer with a mountain's head," "a pheasant with hungry wings," the "jumping sausages, roasting pies/ And long loaves in the bin,/ And a stump of Caerphilly" cheese which they missed getting at the inn, and "a ham-bone high on a ceiling-hook,/ And a goose with a golden skin" which they can see inside (pp. 73, 74, 86).

Unsuccessful at gaining entry, they leave after midnight has struck, chanting:

> It is a skull we carry
> In the ribbons of a bride. (p. 87)

Marie Trevelyan's account of the custom at the beginning of this century validates many extra details of the poem's description:

> The Mari Llwyd was always accompanied by a large party of men, several of whom were specially selected on account of their quick wit and ready rhymes. The mode of proceeding was always the same. All doors in the parish were safely shut and barred when it was known that the Mari Llwyd commenced her itinerary. When the party reached the doors of a house an earnest appeal was made for permission to sing. When this was granted, the company began recounting in song the hard fate of mankind and the poor in the dark and cold days of winter. Then the leading singer would beg those inside to be generous with their cakes and beer and other good things. It was customary for the householder to lament and

plead that, alas! times had been bad with him, and he had little to spare. Then began a kind of conflict in verse, sung or recited, or both. Riddles and questions were asked in verse inside and outside the house. Sarcasm, wit, and merry banter followed, and if the Mari Llwyd party defeated the householder by reason of superior wit, the latter had to open the door and admit the conquerors. Then the great bowl of hot spiced beer was produced, and an ample supply of cakes and other good things. The feast began and continued for a short time, and when the Mari Lwyd moved away the leader found contributions of money in his collecting bag.

Many specimens of the introductory rhymes, the challenge from without, the reply from within, together with the verses sung when the Mari Llwyd entered the house, and afterwards departed, are still preserved and well remembered.[2]

Some allusions that Watkins makes in the Ballad are not covered by his note. So, for example, when the Mari's retinue at the close of the Ballad speaks of "the stiff and stuffed and stifled thing/Gleaming in the sack" (p. 87), we have to go to other accounts of the tradition for enlightenment. Jonathan Ceredig Davies notes that "when a real skeleton could not be got, it was customary to make one of straw and rags," and the man who carried the Mari was "enveloped in a large white sheet."[3] In my own county of Monmouthshire when I was a child, the "stiff, stuffed" horse was made like this:

We had a special arrangement of rods driven into the lower jaw. With these we could make the jaws shut with an awful crunch. We filled the eye-holes with wadding (cotton batting or padding) and "pop-alleys" (glass "shooters" in the game of marbles) and fixed great ears made of wadding stiffened with cardboard; then we stuck rosettes on the sides of the skull and strung long coloured ribbons as reins. . . . One man acted as leader with the ribbons, then came the Mari draped in a white sheet, followed by the three singers.

2 *Folk-Lore and Folk-Stories of Wales* (London, 1909), p. 32. Parenthetical page references to Trevelyan in the text are to this work.
3 *Folklore of West and Mid-Wales* (Aberystwyth, 1911), p. 61. Parenthetical page references to Davies in the text are to this work.
4 Fred J. Hando, *Journeys in Gwent* (Newport, Mon., 1951), p. 23. From a first-hand description by Augustus Sargeant. See also Hando's *The Pleasant Land of Gwent* (Newport, Mon., 1944), p. 101.

The horse's skull or the wooden head was attached to a pole borne by a man hidden either by the sheet or a long robe.

Most authorities agree that the Mari Lwyd must have had a common origin with the Hooden Horse ceremony of Kent conducted in recent times at Christmas by a group of carollers carrying a horse's head or skull. Matching quite closely with the descriptions of the Mari above, and throwing more light on Watkins's "stiff and stuffed and stifled thing/ Gleaming in the sack" (p. 87), is this interesting account of the Hooden Horse:

> In connection with the head is a piece of stout sacking in the shape of a sack. Under this sack-cloth the hoodener conceals himself, so that only his legs are seen.[5]

A piece of information on the Hooden Horse by the author Edward Percy also sheds light on the allusion in the Ballad to the skull of the Mari being decked out "in the ribbons of a bride" (p. 87). Percy reports that the skull, or its wooden facsimile, was "hung with 'ellinge'—a stout hop-stacking, itself wildly decorated with flame-coloured ribbons, bells and housings called 'the caytis.' "[6]

But Watkins has done a great deal more than give us a description of the residual folk rite. The general tone of the Ballad is at clashing odds with the tone of joviality and hilarity which marks modern celebrations of the tradition. What he has done is to revive the terror with which this ancient horse-head custom must originally have been invested when the ritual had real and awesome meaning for the participants.

The etymology of the Kentish work "ellinge" gives some indication of this, as Percy's account reveals:

> As an adjective "ellinge" means solitary, lonely, ghostly. . . . As a noun it was used to describe the sacking covering the bodies of persons supporting the ghastly Hooden Horse, that startling apparition with which the men of Kent were wont to delight and horrify their neighbours at Christmas tide.

---

5 Quoted from an account by Percy Maylam in M. Oldfield Howey, *The Horse in Magic and Myth* (New York, 1958), p. 92. Parenthetical references in Howey in the text are to this work.
6 Quoted by Hando in *Journeys in Gwent,* pp. 24-25.

The mock fright with which modern visitations of the Mari and the Hooden Horse are received (like the "spooks" and "wraiths" received at our doors on another "spirit night," the night of Hallowe'en) also intimates the real fear that once attended the appearance of the horse's skull.

The name alone of the "Mari Lwyd" may be evocative of the supernatural and its attendant fear. In his identification of the Mari Lwyd with the Hooden Horse, Howey translates the name a little differently from the "Grey Mari," of Watkins, explaining the Welsh name as "Pale Mary, Wan Mary, or White Mary" (p. 95). He also gives the alternate spelling of "Llwyd" as in Marie Trevelyan's account above. The basic Welsh adjective "llwyd," which by the process of consonantal mutation is lenated to "lwyd" before a feminine noun, means "grey, pale, hoary." Whether clothed in a white sheet or in the greyish fibre of jute, flax or hemp from which hop-sacking or burlap is made, the Mari suggests the grey-white terror of an apparition, and Watkins's description of her "gleaming in the sack" presumably suggests spectral luminescence. Discussing this terror, Marie Trevelyan speculates that "Mari" may actually be "Marw"—meaning "death" in Welsh (p. 33). The country people would have had reason to flee in terror from the Grey Death.

The Symbolic Values of White in the Ballad and Other Poems

Watkins evokes the terror of the old custom in his poem partly by the multiple use of whiteness, whose symbolic values here appear at first glance to be predominantly the adverse one of negation and absence of life. The insiders at the feast see the white horse as a white ghost; they tell the Mari's retinue to toss her "to the white spray's crest" since "White horses need white horses' food;/We cannot feed a ghost" (p. 75).

Time and place are equally whitely negative; there is the white of night and winter, of sky, land and sea in the following:

> O white is the starlight, white on the gate
> And white on the bar of the door.
> Our breath is white in the frost, our fate
> Falls in the dull wave's roar. (p. 75)

It is the color of the "ash of the grave," of the "white terror" excited by a "white horse's head in the frost," of the "austere star-energies, naked, white" (p. 76) which "make us afraid" (p. 82). It is a white which is cold, remorseless, frightening and dead.

Yet the quality of the whiteness itself is not dead, not flat or mat; it is brilliant. As we have seen, the Mari gleams and shines; she is "white in her starry reins" like the white stars and the white fire light, the glittering Plough, the "starlike fire" and the "stinging light of the stars," as are those in her retinue who are "All lit by phosphorus up" (p. 84).

But there is a paradox: the Mari's white-brightness has the quality of blackness. As she shines in the black of the sack:

> The Mari's shadow is too bright,
> Her brilliance is too black. (p. 87)

And behind this antinomy, incidentally, is a very precise sensory reaction—the effect of staring at a brilliant light is a dark patch on the retina.

Watkins's preoccupation with the paradoxical nature of white is suggestive of Melville's in *Moby Dick*:

> But not yet have we solved the incantation of this whiteness, and learned why it appeals with such power to the soul; and more strange and far more portentous—why, as we have seen, it is at once the most meaning symbol of spiritual things, nay the very veil of the Christian's Deity; and yet should be as it is, the intensifying agent in things the most appalling to mankind.[7]

An estimate of whether Watkins's whiteness is only—to use Melville's words—"the intensifying agent in things most appalling to mankind" (of which, Ishmael concluded, the Albino whale was the symbol); or whether it operates also in the Ballad as "the most meaning symbol of spiritual things" to unify opposites or ambivalences, must wait upon a fuller dis-

---

7 Ch. xlii. See James Baird, *Ishmael* (Baltimore, 1956), pp. 256-277, for a discussion of Melville's "archetypal obsession" with whiteness; and M. O. Percival. *A Reading of Moby-Dick* (Chicago, 1950), p. 57, for a recognition of the symbol of whiteness as a union of opposites of good and evil.

cussion of the nature and origins of the Mari Lwyd below. But a statement by Watkins in "New Year 1965" that his imagination seized on the custom to figure forth a "kind of reconciliation of contraries, an eternal moment of contradictions" (p. 22) not only suggests the antinomy of white-in-black and black-in-white we have already noted in the poem, but intimates a strong presumption that other symbolic values than those of negation attach to whiteness in the Ballad.

Let us go outside the Ballad for a moment to consider a poem published in 1943, which casts more light on Watkins's colour symbolism. In "Music of Colours—White Blossom" (*The Lady with the Unicorn*, pp. 11-12) Watkins explores at length the values of whiteness. Here blossoms and shells partake of sublimity by virtue of the whiteness associated with mystics, religieux and Christ, "who know the music by which white is seen," who are, that is to say, tuned in to celestial music, which is as transfiguring to hear as pure white is to see. This transcendant white is so pure that by contrast the snow of the poles and the Scythian hills no longer merit the term white:

> White blossom, white, white shell; the Nazarene
> Walking in the ear; white touched by souls
> Who know the music by which is seen,
> Blinding white, from strings and aureoles,
> Until that is not white, seen at the two poles,
> Nor white the Scythian hills, nor Marlowe's queen.

How white is pure white? The sea spray and foam appear white until the snowfall dulls it by contrast. This repeated discovery, that what we thought was true white is not really so, may suggest that nothing is white. But Watkins believes that out of the deluge whose end was marked by the rainbow, "an unknown colour is saved," presumably true white, which symbolizes life and light, though it is never manifested in its pure unadulterated form in natural phenomena:

> The spray looked white until this snowfall.
> Now the foam is grey, the wave is dull.
> Call nothing white again, we were deceived.
> The flood of Noah dies, the rainbow is lived.
> Yet from the deluge of illusions an unknown colour is saved.

Now this symbolism of the rainbow's relationship to white, it is interesting to note, has a precise physical foundation. Newton's experiments recombined the spectrum into white light. Newton's disk, sectioned into colours of the spectrum, when spun at a certain speed blends all colours into a luminous white.[8]

While true white is "unknown," unapprehended by the senses, natural white, the imperfect white that can be seized by human eyes, like the entire order of natural colours which the rainbow symbolizes, must, as in the seasonal myth, die into blackness in order to be reborn. We see at once that in Watkins's colour symbolism black is not viewed as negative; on the contrary, the darkness of the inscrutable seed is the repository of purest white, the life stuff, light, which will break anguishedly into nature again, not as pure, ideal white, but as a rainbow of colour of which imperfect white is viewed as a component:

> White must die black, to be born white again
> From the womb of sounds, the inscrutable grain,
> From the crushed, dark fibre, breaking in pain.
>
> The bud of the apple is already forming there.
> The cherry-bud, too, is firm, and behind it the pear
> Conspires with the racing cloud, I shall not look.
> The rainbow is diving through the wide-open book
> Past the rustling paper of birch, the sorceries of bark.

Ironically, even the imperfect whites of nature, of blossom and cloud, the white of the hawthorn bud or may blossom, will not "break," cannot be realized, until their less-than-ideality is acknowledged, or until the existence of ideal white asleep in darkness is recognized:

> Buds in April, on the waiting branch,
> Starrily opening, light raindrops drench,
> Swinging from world to world when starlings sweep,
> Where they alight in air, are white asleep.

8 See Harold Bayley, *The Lost Language of Symbolism* (New York, 1958), II, 55, for mention of this phenomenon, and its mystical implications of many colours unified in the white One.

> They will not break, not break, until you say
> White is not white again, nor may may.

In nature, ironically, that colour closest to the Ideal—to Real White—is the most transient. It is the dark forest, not the lilies, which endures around Solomon's grave:

> White flowers die soonest, die into that chaste
> Bride-bed of the moon, their lives laid waste.
> Lilies of Solomon, taken by the gust,
> Sigh, make way. And the dark forest
> Haunts the lowly crib near Solomon's dust,
> Rocked to the end of majesty, warmed by the low beast,
> Locked in the liberty of his tremendous rest.

True white, Ideal white, is equated with the miraculous power of Christ, who could convert the white corruption of the leper into the white of cleanness. In contrast to this "original whiteness" even lovers' whiteness, "myth's whiteness" — Venus's white doves and the swan-whiteness of Leda and Jove — looks wan. Real white, "transfiguring whiteness" is paradoxically concealed in the black-swan secrecy and darkness of the land of the dead. Only awareness of our lack of it lets us know reality.

> If there is white, or has been white, it must have been
> When His eyes looked down and made the leper clean.
> White will not be, apart, though the trees try
> Spirals of blossom, their green conspiracy.
> She who touched His garment saw no white tree.
>
> Lovers speak of Venus, and the white doves,
> Jubilant, the white girl, myth's whiteness, Jove's,
> Of Leda, the swan, whitest of his loves.
> Lust imagines him, web-footed Jupiter, great down
> Of thundering light; love's yearning pulls him down
> On the white swan-breast, the magical lawn,
> Involved in plumage, mastered by the veins of dawn.
>
> In the churchyard the yew is neither green nor black.
> I know nothing of Earth or colour until I know I lack
> Original white, by which the ravishing bird looks wan.
> The mound of dust is nearer, white of mute dust that dies
> In the soundfall's great light, the music in the eyes,
> Transfiguring whiteness into shadows gone,
> Utterly secret. I know you, black swan.

"Music of Colours: The Blossom Scattered" (*The Death Bell*, pp. 26-28), first published in 1949, continues the exploration of the mystical import of white. The symbolic equations are the same: colours of the rainbow and imperfect white represent transient natural phenomena. Obversely, pure white, original whiteness, the perpetual transcendent life stuff, is seldom experienced by men except in epiphanic moments as at the advent of Christ, and Jove's visitation of Leda, and other moments of miraculous conception and generation, when, "all colours hurled in one," a transfiguring radiance occurs.

Again blackness, darkness, represents death, but certainly not in a negative or destructive sense—rather in that sense of the inscrutable darkness and secretness of the womb of earth which receives and shelters the fallen fruit until it is reborn into the light and colours of earth. In this darkness the force of life and love, Ideal whiteness, is secreted:

. . . white breaks from darkness . . .

And:

> Then the white petal of whitest darkness made
> Breaks and is silent.

The palette of "the world's colours" which "in flashes come and go" are again viewed as pure white broken down into its natural elements—all that man can know of the Ideal, elemental life stuff.

This poem develops more fully the theme of the transience of natural whiteness touched on in the first "Music of Colours" poem. It makes the point that by a strange irony "White of the risen body," the light broken out of darkness, "white from the shadows come," is really only experienced by man through the process of the birth, growth, decay and death of natural phenomena. Paradoxically, it is only by virtue of his finiteness that man can glimpse the infinite; only through experiencing time can he conceive of timelessness:

> Not space revealed it [light, white], but the needle's eye
> Love's dark thread holding, when we began to die.

31

These views, reminiscent of Wallace Stevens's "Death is the mother of beauty" in the poem "Sunday Morning," will be explored more fully in another context below.

Watkins's third poem in his exploration of colour, "Music of Colours—Dragonfoil and the Furnace of Colours" (*Affinities*, p. 80), deals at much greater length with the palette or rainbow of brilliant colours in nature, using the imagery of a summer garden, which, in its "dazzling profusion" is "Sprung from the white fire" and "nurtured of the white light." He parallels this to the "Light, born of white light, broken by the wave's plunge/Here into colours." For "the rainbow/Flying in spray, perpetuates the white light," as much as does the blaze of blossoms.

Here again darkness is the necessary complement, the secret repository where light waits to burst into the "colours of destruction":

>   deep in fume of poppies
> Sleep the black stamens.

But the glory of this "sudden incarnation" of colour is so entrancing that

>   we cannot see that other
> Order of colours moving in the white light.
> Time is for us transfigured into colours . . .

Yet, paradoxically, losing himself so completely in the beauty of these ephemerae, man may glimpse eternity and immortality:

> True for the moment, therefore never dying.

What have these "Music of Colours" poems to do with the "Ballad of the Mari Lwyd"? If there is any consistency in Watkins's vision, they should alert us to tread warily in ascribing to the whiteness of the Mari only adverse connotations. Her gleaming whiteness may incorporate symbolic values of sublimity as well as ghoulish terror; ideality and permanence as well as corruption and transience.

Likewise the blackness of her brilliance, and her too-bright

shadow may suggest a concept of death as a state of regeneration, of constructive interrelationship with life itself, rather
than a purely negative one of termination of life. We must bear
these possibilities in mind as we move through the poem to
reduce the chances of distortion arising from our symbolic
stereotypes and misconceptions.

This is not to suggest that Watkins's symbols are private.
Although he gives them the twist of his own purely personal
vision, their values are consistent with the hermetic tradition.
Black, as in the "germination in darkness" of the black chaotic
original substance in the alembic of the alchemists, seems
generally to represent the precondition or initial stage of
generation, [9] reinforced by the notion of the blackness of the
seed-germinating earth. A rainbow of colour in alchemical lore,
referred to as "the peacock's tail," signifies inception or birth or
rebirth, as when the black germinal substance heated in the
alembic takes on an iridesence. The same equations are
deduced in Jungian psychology:

> The change from black or white to all-colors represents the
> change from death to new life, according to the alternation found
> in the cycle of nature in its archetypal form.[10]

The ambivalence of white in Watkins's work is also in
keeping with colour values in the occult tradition. White may
represent, in "its negative quality of lividness," the value of
death. More often white represents timelessness, ecstasy and
"intuition of the Beyond," according to Cirlot, (p. 55). In the
words of Jungian psychologists:

> This white is an ambiguous colour and would seem to embody just
> that spirit of paradox which is the essence of the death and re-

9 J. E. Cirlot, *A Dictionary of Symbols,* trans. Jack Sage (New York, 1962),
   p. 55. Parenthetical page references to Cirlot are to this work.
10 Joseph L. Henderson and Maud Oakes, *The Wisdom of the Serpent: The
   Myths of Death, Rebirth, and Resurrection* (New York, 1963), pp. 35-36.

birth experience, as if to indicate that white is black as life is death and death is life renewed.[11]

This useful summary will stand us in good stead when we come to evaluate the Ballad *in toto* below.

11 Ibid, p. 34.

CHAPTER III

THE RETINUE IN THE
"BALLAD OF THE MARI LWYD"

The fear associated with the tradition of the Mari Lwyd has been attributed in part to the threat of violence of the riotous throngs which used to accompany the Mari, a violence comparable to the vandalism perpetrated by gangs of Hallowe'en pranksters even in recent times. Marie Trevelyan notes that in some places in the last century, the custom became so degenerate that if demands for refreshments were not met "the men forced an entrance, raked the fire out of the kitchen grate, looted the larder, and committed other depradations" (pp. 32-33).

But to the residents visited by the retinue of the Mari in Watkins's Ballad, the participants are far more frightening than any bunch of marauding hooligans of folk memory or historic record. They are the most terrifying retinue possible: the erected Dead, as the first lines of the Prologue inform us:

> Mari Lwyd, Horse of Frost, Star-horse, and White Horse
> of the Sea, is carried to us.
> The Dead return.
> The Exiles carry her . . . (p. 69)

In the first part of the poem "they tear through the frost of the ground," and with their dead white hands "rip the seams of their proper white clothes" and "the white sheet under the frosted glass" (pp. 74, 70).

Retinues in Celtic Folk Customs and Legends
What is the source of this hair-raising retinue? Is there any-

thing in modern or ancient versions of the custom which could have suggested such a retinue to Watkins, and which would be useful for us to know in our reading of the poem? Watkins's note following the Ballad seems to indicate that his choice was as much a product of his imagination as of anything else. It seems that as his memory recovered details of the custom, his imagination was at work both restoring its original power and significance, and remaking it to convey such metaphysical truths as the poem was written to engage:

> The singers came every year to my father's house; and listening to them at midnight, I found myself imagining a skull, a horse's skull decked with ribbons, followed and surrounded by all kinds of drunken claims and holy deceptions.

> I have attempted to bring together those who are separated. The last breath of the year is their threshold, the moment of supreme forgiveness, confusion and understanding, the profane and sacred moment impossible to realize while the clock hands divide the Living from the Dead. (p. 90)

In his note in "New Year 1965" (p. 22), he says:

> As I listened, it seemed to me that the old custom assumed terrifying proportions, for not only drunken and holy people, but the dead themselves seemed to have come to the house. This, too, was a kind of reconciliation of contraries, an eternal moment of contradictions, and my "Ballad of the Mari Lwyd" began to take shape.

Certainly there is little in recent versions of the custom of the Mari Lwyd, or even in accounts of the last century or so, to suggest a retinue of the Dead. Whether the custom was attached to Christmas or the New Year, the retinue was always made up of revellers. "A merry procession" of carollers, J. Ceredig Davies calls them, "singing songs and playing merry pranks, collecting Christmas boxes," for the "Mari Lwyd Lawen," the Merry Grey Mary (p. 61). In other accounts they generally took part in the festivities of the Twelve Days of Christmas, and in many localities came to be associated exclusively with New Year's revelries. Davies also reports a May Day custom in Pembrokeshire attached to the ceremony of bringing in the grain to the mill when a band of young men and women dress up a horse's head as May Day sport (p. 82).

Marie Trevelyan's work, however, contains accounts of some versions of the custom with unusual retinues which invite speculation. She speaks of one retinue in which "youths bearing brands, and small boys dressed up as bears, foxes, squirrels, and rabbits, helped to swell the throng" (pp. 30-31). In a variant custom called "Aderyn Pig Llwyd"—Bird with the Grey Beak—reminiscent of ceremonies of the Killing of the Wren, a troupe of morris dancers often accompanied the horse's head, these morris dancers being "dressed as gaily and grotesquely as possible," wearing "caps of any kind of animal's skin and short jackets . . . all decorated with gay knots of ribbon. Sometimes the head and brush of a fox were prominent," and sometimes "bells and jingling ornaments were worn round the wrists and ankles, and frequently one or two of the party appeared as Megan, a hag of the night, in female dress" (p. 31).

The animal costumes of these mummers is substantiation for the view, shared by many authorities, that the various horse-head ceremonies in Britain derive from pagan rites involving the worship and/or sacrifice of animals. This view is partly deduced from the process of debasement of the rite in modern times from the use of an actual skull to the substitution of a wooden facsimile, a practice Watkins mentions in his note. In turn, the skull had become, Percy Maylam assumes, "the substitute for the living or newly sacrificed animal, in what was once a solemn religious procession to or from the altar" (Howey, p. 95).

In the same discussion Howey goes on to speculate about the original ritual:

> In the original sacrifices the head and skin were probably used in the ritual to cover the celebrant, as where animals are sacrificed it appears to be a common custom for the priest thus to clothe himself, whilst the worshippers partook with him sacramentally of the flesh of the god-impregnated victim, thus mystically attaining union with the divinity (p. 95).[1]

1 See H. R. Hays, *In the Beginnings* (New York, 1963), p. 156, for an interesting account of the shaman of the Yakut tribe in present-day Siberia inducing his frenzy on a white mare's skin. Hays also cites Geza Roheim, *Animism, Magic and the Divine King* (London, 1930), on the way man can attain union with his god both by coupling with it and eating it, and on man's primal sense of union with animals in totemism. Parenthetical page references in the text are to Hays's *In the Beginnings*.

With the coming of Christianity, these pagan rites were absorbed or suppressed, and Howey reminds us that residual practices were condemned as "demoniacum" in Archbishop Theodore's *Penitential* of 690 A.D., where penances are prescribed for "any who on the kalends of January clothe themselves with the skins of cattle and carry heads of animals" (p. 98). To get around the Christian proscription, perpetuators of the pagan custom thereafter resorted to wearing artificial heads and skins, and to burying the sacred skull of a sacrificed animal for exhumation and repeated use year after year—a practice Watkins notes.

Even so, these early retinues as well as their descendants, the animal-garbed retinues of modern attenuations, were *living* celebrants, and while they explain some of the religious terror which the poem recaptures, they do not, of course, explain Watkins's choice of a retinue of dead men.

There is, however, another Celtic legend still alive in Wales, which links the notion of an animal retinue with the host of the Dead. It is a retinue altogether more terrifying than any band of pranksters carrying the Mari Lwyd of modern form. The Welsh legend in question is of the *Cwn Annwn,* the hounds of Annwn, the pagan Celtic Otherworld. These "hounds of hell," as they are called in their Christianized versions, are "spirit-hounds" "passing through the air in pursuit of objects of their malice." They appear in various terrifying emanations, often ugly, often dripping with gore.

These hounds were heard usually in the dead of night by travellers in lonely districts remote from villages. Sometimes they howled in wild lamentation, or bayed in appalling chorus, usually on the eves of St. John, St. Martin, St. Michael, All Saints, Christmas, the New Year, St. David, or St. Agnes, as they raced in procession through the lonely lands of Wales. Like the Greek Hekate and her mediaeval witches, their favourite meeting-places were cross-roads and graveyards, and

---

2 Trevelyan, p. 47. Summary and quotation in the next few pages concerning this custom come from her account on pp. 47-49, unless otherwise acknowledged.

whenever their feet touched the mandrake, the latter screamed aloud.[3]

Now it is not the Cwn Annwn themselves which appear to form the basis of Watkins's retinue, but the victims and the followers of this ravaging horde. Trevelyan quotes from Edmund Jones of Tranch, "A Relation of Apparitions of Spirits in the Principality of Wales, etc." (Trevecca, 1780), p. 20, that if any person by accident, design, or curiosity joins these hounds, "blood falls in showers like rain, human bodies are torn to pieces, and death soon follows the victim of the nocturnal expedition." She also quotes claims from Charles Redwood's "The Vale of Glamorgan," published anonymously in 1839, p. 300, that these uncanny hounds leave traces of their violence at cross-roads and around graves in the shape of human bones, torn-up turf, and lumps of earth, which, when trodden on, emit "a strong smell of sulphur."

But Trevelyan's most important contribution to understanding Watkins's retinue of the Dead comes from her recording of oral statements summarized and quoted in her study:

It was said in the past that those souls which were not good enough to enter heaven, nor yet bad enough to merit hell, were doomed to ride about following the Cwn Annwn to the end of all time. The cavalcade of doomed souls included "drunkards, scoffers, tricksters, attorneys, parsons' wives, and witches!" (p. 33)

Sir John Rhys, *Celtic Folklore: Welsh and Manx* (Oxford, 1901) I, 216-217, gives a Christianized version of this, remarking (rather tongue in cheek) that the hounds' retinue of souls can only be wicked men: "Their quarry consists of the souls of

3 That the connection between the Cwn Annwn and Hekate is more than casual is suggested by this passage from E. O. James's *The Cult of the Mother-Goddess* (London, 1959), p. 50: "It was doubtless because she ruled over ghosts and demons that she was regarded as the goddess of the cross-roads who drove away the evil influences from these dangerous spots. Therefore, at night under a full moon, ritually prescribed food offerings, known as 'Hecate's suppers,' were placed at the parting of the ways, to placate her if and when she appeared with her hounds of hell."

the departed, and . . . their bark forebodes a death, since they watch for the souls of men about to die. This, however, might be objected to as pagan; so I have heard the finishing touch given to it in the neighbourhood of Ystrad Meurig . . . that it is the souls only of notoriously wicked men and well-known evil livers."

How like this "cavalcade of doomed souls" is Watkins's retinue of the Dead, even to being composed of drunkards, tricksters and evil-doers not quite bad enough to merit eternal damnation. Watkins's Dead are men "with red throats parched for gin/With buckled knuckles and bottle-necked oaths" (p. 74). According to the Living, they are: "Men of the night with a legion of wrongs . . . / Hated lechers with holy songs,/ Bastard bodies that bear no name" (p. 77). They are criminal, gambler and drunkard:

> Listen. Listen. Who comes near?
> What man with a price on his head?
> What load of dice, what leak in the beer
> Has pulled your steps from the dead? (p. 73)

How much closer could we get to the procession of souls Trevelyan reports, and which she described elsewhere as "disembodied spirits who were doomed to everlasting wanderings on earth or in the air," on whom the hounds of hell "were supposed to inflict perpetual torment" (p. 51)? There cannot be much doubt that Watkins knew these legends, and it seems highly probable that the poet Watkins consciously or unconsciously merged these retinues with ancient celebrants and modern revellers of the Mari Lwyd ceremony of folk custom to create his retinue. One detail from Jones of Tranch's account (pp. 28, 29) tends to point to Watkins's knowing synthesis: the nearer the hounds were to mankind, the fainter were their voices; the farther away, the louder they sounded. Is it possible this suggested the diminuendos and crescendos of the retinue's chanting in the Ballad, accounting particularly for the inexplicable loudening of the retinue's final statement after they have left at the very end?

The Cŵn Annwn has a great deal in common with other

spirit retinues in Indo-European myth and folklore. Continental lore contains many variations of the Wild Hunt or Army, a ghostly mounted horde of shrieking, frenzied warriors generally seen on Christmas Eve (the Norse Midwinter festival of Yul), Twelfth Night or Fastnacht. In his discussion of these legends, (pp. 156-159; 170-171), Hays notes that "in some traditions the spirits demand bread and beer, clearly a religious offering." Since this Wild Hunt is often associated with Odin or Woden, it is thereby linked with Odin's assistants in battle, the Valkyries, or "choosers of the slain." These supernatural women in armour and on horseback flew swiftly over land and sea leading the dead warriors back to Valhalla.[4] The combination of equestrian female and a retinue of dead souls is provocative.

Another famous and terrifying retinue of myth, which may have had some bearing on Watkins's retinue of the Dead, is the host of the Greek Hekate. That host of keres or ghosts coursed through the air bringing uncleanness, mischief, nightmares, epilepsy and even insanity in their wake. *Keres* were spirits of the dead which emerged as little winged creatures from Pandora's box, presumably the *pithos* in which ancient Greeks buried their dead.[5] By an association of ideas, the *keres* have been perpetuated in folk lore in the belief that moths and butterflies are bad souls and good souls,[6] a notion which Watkins appears to have incorporated in his Ballad in the lines: "Resurrection's wings and corruption's moth" (p. 83), and "A knock of a moth on the pane of light" (p. 72).

The Celtic Cult of the Dead: The Living Corpse and the Otherworld

In all the retinues discussed so far on which Watkins's retinue

---

4 H. R. Ellis Davidson, *Gods and Myths of Northern Europe* (Baltimore, 1964), pp. 61-62. Parenthetical references to Davidson in the text are to this work.

5 Lewis Bayles Paton, *Spiritism and the Cult of the Dead in Antiquity* (New York, 1921), p. 77. References to Paton are to this work.

6 Ibid., p. 96. See also Rhys, II, 612, for examples of folklore in which souls of the departed are equated with moths and butterflies.

may in part be modelled, the attitude of the Dead towards the Living is understood to be one of unadulterated malice and hostility, and the response of the Living one of dread and rejection. The Greek *keres* are a swarm of evil and mischief. The Cŵn Annwn in Welsh folklore invariably inflict harm on the undeserving and unsuspecting, the more so since most versions have been Christianized into a host of demons led by the devil himself.[7] Successful resistance of this evil force almost always involves Christian prayers or symbols, witness the Merioneth girl who, lost on the mountain, saved herself from the hounds of hell by reciting the Lord's Prayer the night through (Trevelyan, p. 51).

The Living in Watkins's Ballad share this view, and because it is the only view our culture remembers, in the mock-fear of Hallowe'en, and so forth, there is a danger that our reading of the poem will be thereby distorted. It is my experience that Watkins's Dead—their powers and attitudes—owe more to far older Celtic notions of the dead than they do to more recent notions with their emphasis on gloom and harm. An evaluation of the poem ought not to be undertaken without at least taking into account these pagan Celtic beliefs on the subject of death.

The cult of the dead actually predated the emergence and dispersion of the Celtic people by many millennia. As Hays points out, a variety of grave goods in Upper Paleolithic graves (gifts for the dead to use at need) attest to the belief in the conception of the living corpse, the continuation of the individual's life beyond the grave (pp. 37-38). Both fear and love contributed to this special care and treatment; survivors believed their dead capable of both good and harm, but the latter would be inflicted only if the living neglected their duties of providing for the corpse's needs.[8]

The fact that one of these rare paleolithic burials was dis-

---

7 Sir John Rhys, *Celtic Folklore: Welsh and Manx*, I, 217.
8 Sibylle von Cles-Reden, *The Realm of the Great Goddess* (Englewood Cliffs, New Jersey, 1962), p. 11. Parenthetical references to Von Cles-Reden in the text are to this work.

covered in the Paviland Cave in Gower in 1823, a few miles around the coast from Pennard where Watkins made his home, must have been of far more than passing interest to him. As we come to know his metaphysical preoccupations, we can be sure he must have pondered the life and meaning of this "Red Lady," as the skeleton was dubbed, both in relation to his own life and identity, and in relation to all men of all time. He speaks of "her" in several poems, this "youth mistaken for bride/In ochre,"[9] recounting her discovery in "The Red Lady":

> But when one day the picks laid bare
> Bones with the same red ochre dyed
> It seemed they'd hit upon a bride
> Whose burial rites had stained the mould.
> Never was skeleton so old
> In Britain found; but, bones perplex
> Their finders: they mistook her sex.[10]

Shells, more than forty cylindrical rods, and fragments of small ivory rings were among the grave goods left to supply the dead man's continuing needs in this particular cave.[11]

From the Roman conquerors of Gaul and Britain we have some intriguing records of the Celts' perpetuation of some of these Stone Age notions and practices concerning death and immortality. Lucan notes that the Celtic warrior had no fear of death, for "death . . . is but the centre of a long life."[12] There is, in other words, continuity between the worlds of here and there, this world and the other, the natural and the supernatural; and death has no finality. Although Greece and Rome purported to cherish a belief in the continuation of life after death, their dis-embodied shades were nothing like the Celtic belief in the.

9 "Digging the Past," *Fidelities,* p. 87.
10 *Fidelities,* p. 89. The red ochre was probably the ritual sprinkling of red earth found in many such burials, which may have been associated with blood and rebirth.
11 Stewart Williams, *Glamorgan Historian,* III (Cowbridge, Glamorgan, 1966), pp. 123 ff.
12 *Pharsalia,* i. 455 ff. Quoted in Translation in Paton, p. 92; and in Alwyn Rees and Brinley Rees, *Celtic Heritage* (London, 1961), p. 340. Parenthetical references to Rees and Rees in the text are to this work.

persistence of the living man beyond the grave as he was in life in all his human qualities and relations.[13] Nor has the Christian doctrine of the resurrection—the assumption by the soul of a new, incorruptible body adapted for a more meaningful existence[14]—much in common with the Celtic view. Valerius Maximus and other classical writers noted with surprise that the Celt would lend money on a promissory note for repayment in the next world.[15] Diodorus Siculus noted that letters were thrown on funeral pyres for delivery to departed friends,[16] and in some cases friends and kin even threw themselves into the flames in the belief that they would live on in the Otherworld beside their loved ones.[17] For the Celts, as for the Egyptians, the future life was a prolongation of the present; a man would find himself among family and friends doing the things he always did, but in more perfect form. Thus men in Welsh myth who visit the Otherworld retain their flesh-and-blood identity. In the First Branch of *The Mabinogion,* Pwyll enjoys a year of perpetual feasting and pleasure in Annwn, the Otherworld, in his own person[18]

To what extent does Watkins's poem hold true to these primitive Celtic notions of the living corpse? As we have seen, his retinue of the Dead are flesh-and-blood creatures; at least they can see, be seen, knock, talk, walk, and they have all the appetites of men. Before we even meet them, the Prologue makes clear that they are not going to be in the Christian tradition, as this parody of Paul's doctrine of the resurrection[19] suggests:

13 T. W. Rolleston, *Myths and Legends: The Celtic Race,* (Boston, n.d.), pp. 78-80.

14 For discussion, see Paton, p. 296.

15 *Factorum et Dictorum Memorabilium Libri Novem,* ii.6.10. Quoted in translation in Nora K. Chadwick, *The Druids,* (Cardiff, 1966), p. 54.

16 V. 28. Quoted in translation in Paton, p. 92.

17 Paton, p. 132.

18 Trans. Gwyn Jones and Thomas Jones (London, 1949), pp. 5 ff.

19 I Corinthians 15:42-58, especially v. 52 and v. 53. "In a moment, in the twinkling of an eye, at the last trump: for the trumpet shall sound and the dead shall be raised incorruptible, and we shall be changed. For this corruptible must put on incorruption, and this mortal must put on immortality."

> They who seem holy and have put on corruption, they who seem
> corrupt and have put on holiness.

They are neither incorruptible bodies nor demons, but a mixed
bag, as we have noted, of heretic, drunkard, thief, and "locked-
out lepers with haloes" (p. 71). If they seem evil, Watkins suggests, it may be because the Living have scorned and neglected
them: "cast them out from their own fear, from their own fear of
themselves, into the outer loneliness of death" (p. 69), forgotten
their community with the dead. And if the Living *have* in-
curred the hostility of the Dead, it is by their own neglect for
having reduced fossil, wraith and ghost to the status of "refuse
cast by the righteous waves" (p. 70), a neglect which in ancient
Celtic belief justly merited the antipathy of the dead.

It is important to realize that Watkins was not just arbi-
trarily reviving these pagan views. In Celtic areas these ancient
beliefs have hung on tenaciously in the lore of the people, despite all Christian efforts to uproot them. Evidence of this
among the Amorican Bretons was turned up in the researches
of A. Le Braz in *La Légende de la Mort* (Paris, 1893), and
similar remnants of the belief have been found in parts of
Wales. In a letter to W. Y. Evans-Wentz, Le Braz observed:

> In truth, in the Breton mind the dead are not dead; they live a
> mysterious life on the edge of real life, but their world remains
> fully mingled with ours, and as soon as night falls, as soon as the
> living, properly so-called, give themselves up to the temporary
> sleep of death, the so-called dead again become the inhabitants of
> the earth which they have never left. They resume their place at
> their former hearth, devote themselves to their old work, take an
> interest in the home, the field, the boat.[20]

Both sides of the Channel Evans-Wentz found a vigorous
belief in apparitions, phantom-funerals and death-warnings
based on the strong conviction that dead men can show themselves at will. "We believe that the spirits of our ancestors sur-
round us and live with us," one peasant declared. Another said:
"Following my own idea, I believe that after death the soul
always exists and travels among us" (pp. 214, 215). Many
personal accounts of the dead incarnating have been collected.

20 Translated in *The Fairy-Faith in Celtic Countries* (New York, 1966), pp.
193-194. Parenthetical references to Evans-Wentz in the text are to this
work.

For the reader to regard the retinue of the Dead in the Ballad with patronizing indulgence, or to assume that such was Watkins's attitude and tone, would lead to serious violation of the poem. No claim is made about Watkins's personal convictions respecting these views. My main concern here is to obstruct a judgement of "quaintness" which would do damage to the reading.

Various allusions in Watkins's poem require some knowledge, too, of the Celtic conception of the Otherworld. In line with the belief in the materiality and continued existence of the corpse, the Celtic Otherworld was not, like the Christian, located in some distant unknown region above the clouds. It was here on earth. It might be *Other,* but it was still *of* this world, the dead continuing to experience the sensations they had known in life, except that they had known in life, except that they were sensations of delight and satisfaction only, without change and without end.

There was no fixed geographical location of this Otherworld. It was sometimes conceived as a subterranean world, hidden under hills, entered through caverns, as in the case of the dwellings of the Irish Sidhe folk. In fairy-lore it is often under a lake. The Welsh Annwn or Annwyfn, the Otherworld kingdom ruled by Arawn, where Pwyll spent a year of perpetual feasting, may have been located in the Prescelly Mountains of Pembrokeshire, the highest and westernmost point in South Wales, and the holy place from which the sacred blue stones of Stonehenge are said to have been transported.

But most often, the Otherworld is located on an island in the Western Ocean. As in Babylonian and Egyptian myth, the Dead were believed to sail through the Gate of the West across the sea to the Abode of the Dead. The palace of Manannan Mac Lir was said to be located in the middle of the Western Ocean, and stories of magic islands abound in Welsh legend, often identified by modern commentators as Bardsey, Grassholm and Lundy, "three outstanding lonely islands off the western coasts of North Wales, South Wales and Cornwall."[21] In the

21 Roger Sherman Loomis, *Wales and the Arthurian Legend* (Cardiff, 1956), p. 146. Parenthetical references to Loomis in the text are to this work.

Second Branch of *The Mabinogion,* the gallant company of Bran retire with his head for a period of feasting to the Island of Gwales in Penfro;[22] and in the Arthurian Romances, it is the island of Avalon or Avilion to which Arthur's body is rowed in a barge to sojourn in timeless perfection pending his return. [23]

The belief in an island Otherworld to which the dead journeyed across water persisted even when the optimistic view of death gave way to a more gloomy, pessimistic view of the afterlife. John Arnott MacCulloch notes Pliny's assertion that the Celtic tribe the Cimbri called the northern sea *"Morimarusam-Mortuum Mare* or possibly *Mortuorum Mare* ('Sea of the Dead')—the sea which the dead crossed."[24] MacCulloch also notes that:

> The supposed Celtic belief in an island of the dead might also explain why, according to Pliny, no animal or man beside the Gallic ocean dies with a rising tide—a belief still current in Brittany; the dead could be carried away only by an outflowing tide.[25]

In the sixth century the Byzantine historian Procopius said fishermen and farmers on the coast of the Continent were exempt from taxes because they had the job of ferrying souls over to "Brittia," each in turn. At midnight they hear a knocking at the door and muffled voices, but when they reach the shore they find only unfamiliar empty boats. After setting out in these, they see the gunwale drop close to the water as though the boats have become heavily laden. Normally taking a day, the journey takes only an hour. As the boats are invisibly unladen, a disembodied voice asks each soul his name and country.[26]

This belief still survives in Brittany (as in parts of Wales). There are several uninhabited and mist-shrouded islands off the coast of Brittany to which the spirits of the dead are thought to

22 Trans. Jones and Jones, p. 39.
23 As in Sir Thomas Malory's *Morte D'Arthur.*
24 *The Mythology of All Races,* III, Celtic (New York, 1964), p. 17. Parenthetical page references to MacCulloch are to this work.
25 Ibid. (Pliny, *Historia Naturalis,* iv. 13.).
26 Ibid., p. 16. (Procopius, *De Bello Gothico,* ii, 566.).

return nightly in the *bag noz,* the "ghost boat"—islands such as Gavr'inis, "goat island," which, according to Sibylle von Cles-Reden, became a residence for living corpses four thousand years or more ago, and seem always to have been avoided by the living as if taboo (p. 241).

Such legends are helpful in understanding various claims and commands made by the Living to the Dead in Watkins's Ballad about whence the Dead have come, and where they should return. The Living charge that the Dead are "brought by the wicked spray" (p. 76), and when the Dead seem to retire at the end of the first "movement" of the poem, they remark:

> Hark, they are going; the footsteps shrink,
> And the sea renews her cry. (p. 76)

When the Dead return, the Living command:

> Go back, with your drowned and drunken eyes
> And your crooked mouths so small
> . . . .
> Go back to the seawave's fall. (p. 81)

One of the Living also conceives of the Dead as "pulling the Plough from the shore" (p. 72), which perhaps suggests a wagon pulled out of the ocean. The constellation of Ursa Major (in various mythologies conceived of as a chariot, a wain, a bier or a coffin),[27] being positioned close to the horizon, suggests emergence from the sea. The command of the Living that the "ghost" white horse, the Mari Lwyd, be tossed to the waves (p. 75), may also conform to the Procopius legend.

There is no inconsistency in the fact that the immediate point of origin of the Dead in Watkins's Ballad was a shroud in a coffin in a grave dug "in the black of the churchyard yew" (p. 79), surmounted by a burial stone. In the cult of the dead, the grave, the tomb and the menhir were venerated as the abode of the dead from which they incarnated, and to which they retired after circulating among the living; and this specific location of their shelter in no way invalidated belief in the Otherworld. This paradox was sustained in most primitive cults without any sense of conflict or contradiction (Paton, p. 99).

27 Gertrude Jobes and James Jobes, *Outer Space* (New York, 1964), p. 265.

For the most part, direct reference to the Otherworld in Watkins's poem is in Christian terms. Annwn (the attractive pagan Other place) has become Hell. "Go back to your Hell, there are clean souls here," the Living scold (p. 86); and the Dead, running out of ammunition, hurl back these prejudices of the Living as a threat:

> Hell curse this house for a badger's holt
> If we find no man devout.
> God singe this doorway, hinge and bolt,
> If you keep our evil out. (p. 83)

The other places that the Dead claim they have come from, Harlech's waves, Engedi, Cader Idris and so forth, are references to their lives-in-life, as well as to the journey across time and space, which, as we shall see later, relates to the nature of the Mari Lwyd. There is no mention of Avalon, the Blessed Isle, or Annwn.

But the poem does contain some references to "glass" which may suggest Otherworld associations. As Loomis points out, "one of the most persistent elements in the Welsh concept of the Other World" (p. 161) is the tradition of a "structure of glass." The glass structure is almost always associated with that other persistent element—an island. The abode of the magician-bard Myrddin, or Merlin, is supposed to have been a house of glass on the island of Bardsey or Ynys Enlli,[28] and either he, or Taliesin, the famous bard, is reputed to have taken the Thirteen Treasures of the Isle of Britain from Caerleon-on-Usk to that Glass House.[29] Chretien de Troyes preserves this mythical reference when he speaks of Maheloas as "the lord of the Isle of Glass; in that isle one hears no thunder, nor does lightning fall there . . ."[30] A false etymology identified Inis Gutrin (Isle of Glass) and Caer Wydr (Glass Castle) with Glastonbury, where

28 Rhys, II, 440; see also his "Hibbert Lectures," quoting from the ancient saga of Merlin, published by the English Text Society, p. 693.
29 According to Edward Jones, *Bardic Museum* (London, 1802), p. 47, quoted in translation by Loomis, p. 160.
30 *Erec*, Ed. W. Foerster (Halle, 1890), 1946 ff. See Loomis, pp. 166-167.

Arthur's soul was said to be housed.[31] Graves contends that the glass coffin in which Snow White is laid as if dead, atop a wooded hill, is "the familiar glass-castle where heroes go to be entertained by the Goddess-of-Life-in-Death," who Snow White, he argues, really is (p. 421).

Does Watkins have something akin to these associations in mind when he speaks of the dead "Ripping the stitch of grief,/The white sheet under the frosted glass" (p. 70), of the "knock of the sands on the glass of the grave" (p. 72)—with a double entendre on "glass" here—and of the Living and the Dead beating with the self-same heart "In the coffin-glass and the window-pane" (p. 77)? The line "Dead men pummel the panes outside" (p. 76), repeated several times in the Ballad, seems to suggest that Watkins conceives of the literal glass of the windows in this poem as the symbolic division between life and death.

It should also be noted that Watkins, in describing the Mari Lwyd's excursion across space and time, to be discussed below, notes that she "has known the room of glass" (p. 77), the Other-world, as well as all places of this world. We should note here Graves's view that "the 'glass' castles of Irish, Manx and Welsh legend are seen to be either island shrines, surrounded by glassy-green water, or star-prisons islanded in the dark-blue night sky."[32] If the room of glass is in the sky, then it might be the "four-square castle of glass" of Arianrhod, namely the counstellation Corona Borealis, to which the souls of dead kings were supposed to repair to await resurrection. What better means to transport them than the Plough, Ursa Major, symbol of the frozen north, which pivots around the Pole and has been known throughout the ages as a vehicle of the dead generally, especially of heroes and kings? Indeed, the Great Bear itself reverberates with Otherworld associations, being

31 See Graves, p. 109. Also Loomis, pp. 166-167.
32 P. 109. He points out that the Saxon word "glas" the equivalent of the Latin "vitrinus" "covered any shade between deep blue and light-green—it could be applied equally to Celtic blue enamel and Roman bottle-glass." He might have added that the Welsh word "glas" means "blue, pale, green, gray."

associated with the polar whiteness of the mythic "Peerless Land" of Thule, which has been called "the white island," identical with the "white mountain," of the Isle of the Blessed (Cirlot, p. 323). But more will be said of this below in a discussion of the Mari Lwyd as "Star-horse" and "Horse of Frost."

Time and Season in the Cult of the Dead

Pagan Celtic notions concerning the cult of the Dead also govern the time and season of the action in Watkins's drama. Let us review these and see to what creative use Watkins has put them.

It is well known even by modern materialists that there are special times when the supernatural world seems closer than usual to the natural world. Given the fundamental duality of night and day, it would make sense to the primitive mind that the living should walk and work in the light, retiring at sundown to their homes, and getting up again at sunrise, and that the dead should be more active at night, retiring, like Hamlet's father's ghost, to rest in their own abode of the Otherworld at cock-crow. In the countryside of Wales, Ireland and Brittany, respect for the fairies and the dead is still used as an argument for retiring early and not keeping abroad at all hours. Because of the association of the night with the Otherworld, persons born in the hours of darkness are said to be able to see ghosts and phantoms invisible to day-born people.[33] For the same reason, the night is the time for wakes for the dead, for the telling of supernatural tales, and for divination, prophecy and witchcraft.

Moreover, within the hours of darkness there are times when the power of the dead is especially concentrated. Midnight, the witching hour, is the time when fairies and phantoms, who have hourly, since sundown, approached the house to check that the coast is clear, become visible, and the living are advised to steer clear of churchyards and fairy mounds. For as Rees and Rees

33 T. Gwynn Jones, *Welsh Folklore and Folk-Custom* (London, 1930), p. 196. Also Rees and Rees, p. 83.

point out, in the old Celtic faith divisions in time have a meaning beyond the purely temporal one (p. 92). At the point where the old day ends and the new day begins, the veil between this world and the unseen world is very thin, and for an instant an opening appears allowing the two worlds to touch (Hays, p. 161).

The belief in the witching hour of midnight is an instance of the archetypal concept of the magical state of "inbetweenness" fundamental to Celtic psychology, a state which Patrick Crampton calls "a chink . . . in the armour of the everyday world leading through to the supernatural," and a condition in which magical happenings are "delicately insinuated between alternatives."[34] Temporal points of inbetweenness are sunrise, sundown, midday, and midnight; spatial chinks occur at fences, boundary lines and thresholds, accounting for the many superstitions still attaching to these times and places. Sexual ambiguity in shamanistic practice, and the changing of sex roles in various folk customs, exemplify the same phenomenon.[35]

Although Watkins says in "New Year, 1965," (p. 22), that "it was just before midnight" that he "caught the sound of a broadcast of the Mari Lwyd ceremony" which triggered his Ballad, it was clearly not simple faithfulness to fact that dominated his choice of time for his action. His imagination clearly seized on the associations of the witching hour and of this magic state of inbetweenness to give the Mari and her retinue a dimension quite lacking in the modern celebrations of the rite. The Prologue suggests to us the awesomeness and terror of the moment of midnight:

34 *Stonehenge of the Kings* (New York, 1968), p. 17.
35 The same phenomenon is at work in such neither-nor-riddles as in the *Third Branch* of *The Mabinogi* where Lleu Llaw Gyffes tells his Delilah-like wife Blodeuwedd that he cannot be slain "within a house nor without," "on horseback nor on foot," but only in a bath by the side of a river, with one foot on a buck and the other on the edge of a roofed-over cauldron or tub. (Trans. Jones and Jones, p. 70). For various other examples, see Rees and Rees, pp. 89 ff., and Kenneth Hurlstone Jackson, *The International Popular Tale and Early Welsh Tradition* (Cardiff, 1961).

Midnight is burning like a taper. In an hour, in less than an hour, it will be blown out.

It is the moment of conscience.

The living moment.
The dead moment.
Listen. (p. 69)

Throughout the Ballad time ticks its relentless way up to the divide, the chink, the mystic boundary, through which this world and the other will touch. The opening lines serve as a refrain which is repeated thirty-nine times, the last time to close the poem:

Midnight. Midnight. Midnight. Midnight.
Hark at the hands of the clock.

Just as in the twenty-four-hour cycle darkness belongs to the dead, so in the cycle of the year is winter their special season. Accounting in part for this is the archetypal myth of the seasons—the death of the star-son and his descent to the underworld—born of primitive awareness of the natural rhythm of the year: fall of leaf and hibernation of seed and animal.

There are also sociological foundations for associating the winter with the cult of the dead:

During the summer, life becomes secular as among the Eskimo. In contrast the coming of winter sees it lived, so to speak, in a continuing religious exaltation. This is the time to celebrate tribal rites, the initiation of adolescents into the tribe's traditions, its beliefs, into the rights and obligations of adults; the time, too, for magical ceremonies to multiply the useful animals, to destroy the great carnivores and to bewitch the game.[36]

It is the time for the shaman to make contact with the spirits, for the artist to decorate cave and sanctuary with his representations of masked figures and beasts, and for the poet to spin tales, spells and incantations.

36 Translated from Henri Breuil and Raymond Lantier, *Les Hommes de la Pierre Ancienne* (Paris, 1959), in Hays, p. 40.

53

If in the twenty-four-hour cycle the joint between the old day
and the new is the point when the dead and living are closest, it
follows that in the cycle of the year, the joint between the old
and the new years is the most supernaturally significant. Again,
as in his use of the witching hour, Watkins clearly saw the
associative potentials of the celebration of this modern remnant
of an ancient rite as part of the revelries of New Year's Eve.

But just as Watkins's retinue is no modern band of merry-
makers, nor even the ritual celebrants of the original rite, his
conception of the passing of the old year into the new is a good
deal more significant than the values we attach to the instant in
modern celebrations. It is probably safe to say that Watkins's
imagination replaced the New Year of the Gregorian calendar
with the rich associations circulating about the Old Celtic New
Year. There is no intention here to suggest that that was when
the Mari Lwyd was originally celebrated. The best bet is that it
was celebrated in its heyday at the Winter Solstice (about
December 22) and was absorbed (much as the Norse Yul) into
the Christian and secular festivals of Christmas and the New
Year. For the Winter Solstice would be the time to celebrate the
turn of the sun back to life, light and growth, the rebirth of the
star son. But it seems likely that Watkins's syncretistic imagination merged the context of the Celtic turn of the year from light
to dark, summer to winter, for the particular metaphysical
values he wished to reveal.

The Celtic New Year is one of the "Nos Ysbrydion," the spirit
nights, perhaps the most active night in the year for supernatural manifestations. The shrewd strategy of the Church is
once more in evidence in its absorption of the pagan festival
into All Hallows Eve, or Hallowe'en. But in Wales "Nos cyn
gaeaf" (night before winter), "Nos yr hen Calan Gaeaf" (night
of the old first day of winter), or simply "Calan gaeaf" (the
calends, or first day of winter) is still the preferred title. The
Celtic quarters of the year did not correspond to the cardinal
points of the sun, but to the cross-quarters, the great feasts cen-
tering around November 1, February 1, May 1, and August 1,
which accounts for the turn coming between October 31 and
November 1. In the old Celtic reckoning of time, as borne out,

Rees and Rees contend (pp. 83-89) by the Coligny calendar (a Gaulish calendar engraved on a bronze tablet unearthed in France in 1897), the year consisted of two halves, summer and winter, even as the day consisted of the two halves of light and dark. The first of May, the Calends of Summer, was called Beltaine; the first of November, the Calends of Winter, was called Samaine or Samain. In May, the young people left the protection of the homestead to take the sheep and other livestock to summer pasture in the hills; before November, at the first frost or snow, they returned to the homestead to pen the livestock in folds and spend the dark months at home crafts and amusements. On Samain the stones rolled back from the tombs and the dead walked, remnants of this belief lingering in the folklore of ghosts, witches and fairies appearing on this night. In modern Wales, mild forms of divination are still practiced, often involving fruit with strong Otherworld associations—the apple and the hazelnut. Apple peel thrown over the shoulder may reveal the name of the prospective husband. Success or failure in bobbing for nuts or apples in water provides answers to questions posed about the future. Spirits of loved ones—prospective or departed—are glimpsed in mirrors, glass being the mystical substance forming, as we have noted, the abode of the privileged dead, and representing symbolically the division between the living and the dead—the invisible veil or barrier.

Welsh customs of recent times attesting to a continuing belief in the ancient conception of the living corpse, its materiality, and its continuing physical needs, included the placatory food offerings on "spirit nights" called *bwyd cennad y meirw,* reminiscent of Hekate's suppers in ancient Greece. To avert harm, and attract the good offices of the dead, hearths were swept, and doors left unbolted to show a welcome, according to T. Gwynn Jones (p. 152). Failure to propitiate the dead might mean the escape of one's horse, the curdling of the milk and similar calamities. If necessity kept one out of doors, it was wise to steer clear of graveyards and to refrain from looking behind if the bushes stirred, especially if the baying of hounds was heard.

These ancient Celtic beliefs relating to the celebration of Samain and the Return of the Dead, which still linger in folk customs in Brittany and Wales, were undoubtedly syncretized in Watkins's imagination. The Breton customs of "the procession of the charnel-house" and "the singers of the dead" seem particularly to have served as important sources of Watkins's Retinue of the Dead, and must be considered in conjunction with those sources offered earlier in this chapter. Indeed, Sir James Frazer's account of these Breton rites (based partly on Le Braz's studies) may have suggested to Watkins other details for his Ballad, including the feast, the white cloth, and the blazing fire. For this reason the passage is quoted at length:

> Similar beliefs as to the annual return of the dead survive to this day in many parts of Europe and find expression in similar customs. The day of the dead or of All Souls, as we call it, is commonly the second of November. Thus in Lower Brittany the souls of the departed come to visit the living on the eve of that day. After vespers are over, the priests and choir walk in procession, "the procession of the charnel-house," chanting a weird dirge in the Breton tongue. Then the people go home, gather round the fire, and talk of the departed. The housewife covers the kitchen table with a white cloth, sets out cider, curds, and hot pancakes on it, and retires with the family to rest. The fire on the hearth is kept up by a huge log known as "the log of the dead" (*kef ann Anaon*). Soon doleful voices outside in the darkness break the stillness of night. It is the "singers of death" who go about the streets waking the sleepers by a wild and melancholy song, in which they remind the living in their comfortable beds to pray for the poor souls in pain. All that night the dead warm themselves at the hearth and feast on the viands prepared for them. . . . In the Vosges Mountains on All Souls' Eve the solemn sound of the church bells invites good Christians to pray for the repose of the dead. While the bells are ringing, it is customary in some families to uncover the beds and open the windows, doubtless in order to let the poor souls enter and rest. No one that evening would dare to remain deaf to the appeal of the bells. (*Adonis, Attis, Osiris*, II, 69),

As the old beliefs clashed with Christianity in Celtic countries, the doubly potent supernatural boundary between day and night and summer and winter was marked by a spirit of mischief and confusion, degenerating in recent customs to personification of the spirits, the masking and blackening of faces, and the wearing of clothing of the opposite sex. Rees and Rees observe:

> A period of disorder in between the old year and the new is a common feature of New Year rituals in many lands, but it is soon followed by the re-creation of an orderly world which lasts for another year. At Hallowe'en the elimination of boundaries, between the dead and the living, between the sexes, between one man's property and another's, and, in divinations, between the present and the future, all symbolize the return of chaos. (p. 91)

It is precisely this misrule, this reversal of order, which the Living in Watkins's Ballad feel:

> Resurrection's wings and corruption's moth
> Beat on the window-pane.
> The tombs are ripped like a table-cloth,
> And madmen teach the sane.
> A voice redresses those ancient wrongs
> With a wrong more deep than all.
> Holy Charity's bastard songs
> Burst from a seawave's fall.   (p. 83)

As in the story of the Mac Oc, Day and Night of Samain serve as a microcosm of all time. Samain serves, too, to remind man of the awful imminence of death, and man's powerlessness at the hands of remorseless time which brings night, winter and death before the rebirth of day, summer and resurrection. Watkins's midnight at the turn of the year is invested with this same awesome import. Several decades after his Ballad, in "New Year, 1965," he wrote:

> The last night of the year is, then, for me, a night of great mystery, even when it breaks into the chiming of the clock and the noise of the bells that announce the New Year. After this, all is lost in greetings and tumultuous singing. The ritual of the Mari Lwyd disappears, and gay processions and dancing take its place. But before all is expectation and the movement of time to its climax, the movement of the refrain of my ballad:
>
> Midnight. Midnight. Midnight. Midnight.
> Hark at the hands of the clock.

Undoubtedly that moment of climax was in some sense "out of the hands of the clock" for Watkins, the *nunc stans* behind the *nunc fluens,* the still point of the turning world behind the "now" which is ever-moving, *il punti a cui tutti le tempi son presenti,* wherein all of time is wrapped up in a ball. Such a moment suggests the same kind of mystery and significance as that moment, that twinkling of an eye, at the last trump when the dead shall be raised incorruptible, and we shall be changed (I Corinthians, 16.53).

All of the background lightly sketched in these chapters was in Watkins's bloodstream, which is why those born outside the tradition cannot expect fully to experience his poem without feeling their way into the context out of which he wrote. When we understand some of these Celtic notions respecting time and the dead, we can better understand how his imagination seized on the explosive possibilities of bringing together "those who are separated," for whom, as he tells us in his Note to the Ballad, "the last breath of the year is their threshold, the moment of supreme forgiveness, confusion and understanding, the profane and sacred moment impossible to realise while the clock hands divide the Living from the Dead (p. 90)."

In this moment of "reconciliation of contraries" Watkins's vision encompassed both the sacrilegious and the sacred, the secular and the holy, the deceptive and the true, the blameworthy and the praiseworthy, the black and the white, the white and the black, the pagan and Christian, the living and the dead, the past and the future. For Samain, above all, reminds man of his community with the past and with the dead, in short of the continuity of his humanity, and this has everything to do with Watkins's metaphysical position as we shall see.

CHAPTER IV

THE SOURCE AND NATURE OF
WATKINS'S MARI

The last of the *dramatis personae* of Watkins's Ballad is the Mari Lwyd, the horse's head who leads the retinue of the Dead, and is described as:

> A stiff, a star-struck thing
> Blown by the stinging spray
> And the stinging light of the stars . . .   (p. 77)

What is she, this "white, stiff thing," who takes no part in the drama either in word or action, yet is so central to it?

In natural terms she is an inanimate object, either a wooden representation of the head of a white horse, or a horse's skull. But in symbolic terms she must be more, in view of her position in the drama. Is she a totem? The facsimile of a sacrificed animal? The emblem of a deity?

Certainly she must have more-than-ordinary attributes and powers, this "Horse of Frost, Star-horse, and White Horse of the Sea," for why else would her epithets and pronouns merit capitalization? Moreover, a good deal of the case which the Dead make for being admitted and entertained by the Living depends on their claims of the Mari Lwyd's godlike qualities, such as omniscience and ubiquity:

> For She knows all from the birth of the Flood
> To this moment where we stand . . .   (p. 74)

In the middle "movement" of the poem, an exchange in quatrains between the Dead and the Living (a section which will be analyzed more fully below) deals exclusively with the Dead's claims for the Mari's power and holiness, and the repudiation by the Living of those claims. Who are we to believe? Is she Mary, Mother of God, or at least one of the other Marys present at Christ's crucifixion as her retinue seems to suggest here:

'Great light you shall gather,
For Mari here is holy;
She saw dark thorns harrow
Your God crowned with the holly.'   (p. 78)

Or does the distinction which the Dead make by using the expression "Your God" set her apart from the Christian tradition? Is, then, the mystery and terror she generates derived from an evil rather than a sacred nature, and are the Living wise to give the Dead's claims no more weight than blowing and fading snow? Which group, if either, does Watkins want us to believe?

Speaking of the imaginative genesis of the work, Watkins says he envisaged the skull "followed and surrounded by all kinds of drunken claims and holy deceptions" (p. 90), and that the Retinue tried to gain entry "on the *pretext* of blessing, *boasting* of the sanctity of what they carried" (p. 89. Italics mine). Does Watkins mean us to give credit only to the claims of the Living? Or should we be wary of committing the intentional fallacy here?

To help settle these questions, we ought perhaps first to inquire into the sources of the Mari of tradition—as we did in the case of sources for the Retinue of the Dead—to see what light they can throw on the Mari Watkins created, treading warily lest these extrinsic materials distort more than illuminate the poem.

The Mari's Relationship to Arawn, the Welsh
Brenin Llwyd, and the Norse Odin

Do the legends and lore we discussed in tracing Watkins's sources for his Retinue of the Dead have anything to tell us about the identity and nature of the Mari? Applying the parallel of the Dead with the Cŵn Annwn, what would that make the Mari?

Marie Trevelyan reminds us (p. 50) that folklore's "hounds of hell" belong to Arawn, the King of Annwn, the Otherworld, whom we meet in the First Branch of *The Mabinogion*. Pwyll, Prince of Dyfed, is out hunting when he hears "the cry of other hounds, a cry different from his own, and coming in the opposite direction."[1] These hounds are different from any Pwyll has seen before. Then he "saw a horseman coming towards him on a large, light-grey steed, with a hunting horn round his neck, and clad in garments of grey woollen in the fashion of a hunting garb."

The grey horse and the grey attire of the king leading these Hounds of Annwn indicate some promising connections with Watkins's Grey Mare, despite the sexual discrepancy. We learn of even more potential links between the Mari and the Grey King in Marie Trevelyan's accounts of the perpetuation of the Arawn myth in Welsh folklore:

> In some parts of Wales it was stated that Arawn and his Cŵn Annwn hunted only from Christmas to Twelfth Night, and was always accompanied by a howling wind. (p. 48)

His greyness persists:

> In Glamorgan, Brecon, and Radnor, Arawn, the master of these hounds rides a grey horse and is robed in grey. (p. 53)

And:

> Stories about the Brenin Llwyd, the Grey King, or Monarch of the Mist, were told in most of the mountainous districts. . . . He was represented as sitting among the mountains, robed in grey clouds and mist. (p. 69)

The mountains he haunted included Cader Idris, mentioned in the Ballad.

The Mari's greyness, the epithet *Lwyd*, her association with the freezing cold (the howling wind and mists) of winter, her equestrian association, the fact that Watkins's action is set within the Twelve Days of Christmas, plus the affinities of the Retinue of the Dead with the Cŵn Annwyn, make it likely that Watkins's imaginative conception owes something to the Brenin Llwyd, Arawn.

R. S. Loomis believes that Pwyll's descent to Annwn at Arawn's behest to fight Hafgan ("Summer White," or "Summer

1 Trans. Lady Charlotte Guest (London, 1910), pp. 13-14.

Sunshine") is no less than the archetypal myth of the seasons, and that "the Grey Huntsman was first created by the imagination of our European ancestors as an embodiment of Storm and Winter" (p. 83). If Watkins's New Year incorporates, as has been suggested above, the values of the Celtic First Night of Winter, then his Mari may also be understood to be an embodiment of Winter, at least as one aspect of her Otherworld identity. One of her titles, "Horse of Frost," the refrain of "horse's head in the frost," the description of her as "Our white, stiff thing,/Death and breath of the frost" (p. 77), and the following account of her as she leaves, support this view:

> O white is the frost on the breath-bleared panes
> And the starlike fire within,
> And our Mari is white in her starry reins
> Starved through flesh and skin. (p. 87)

It should be noted here, perhaps, that the Anglo-Welsh dialect word "to starve"—from Anglo-Saxon *steorfan*, to die, perish—is used to describe dying by cold as well as dying by hunger.

This Welsh "Grey Huntsman," the Brenin Llwyd, Arawn, is identified with the Norse god Odin or Woden, the Grey or Wild Huntsman of Continental lore.[2] The Cult of Odin is associated with horse rites and sacrifices reflected in the Hooden Horse ceremonies of Kent, with which, as has already been noted, the Mari Lwyd of Welsh tradition is linked. Odin was not only propitiated and invoked by celebration of rites involving horse sacrifice; it is hinted in myth and lore that he himself actually possessed the attributes of the horse killed in his honour. He was also conceived of, according to Snorri, as wandering the earth through the air on his eight-legged steed Sleipnir, whom the trickster Loki had foaled while he was in mare's shape.[3]

These equine associations strengthen the possibility of the Mari's linkage to Odin, and it may be helpful to consider how the horse functions in the Odin myth. One explanation of why Odin was himself often thought of as a horse might be given in

2 See Loomis, p. 83; Graves, p. 321; Rhys, I, 143.
3 Davidson, pp. 140-149, 178.

terms of totemism—Odin being a creative spirit, half-animal, half-human, responsible for the creation and perpetuation of the tribe. There is also in the cult of Odin a strong presumption of shamanism, shaman being the term the Russians have given to primitive magicians who invoke the spirits, and which has come to be used generally in anthropology for the ecstatic sorcerer (Hays, pp. 413-414). The possession by, identification with, or transformation into, animal shape during the ritual trance or frenzy through which contact is made with the spirit world is a hallmark of shamanism, and the shape-changing characteristic of the Norse gods must surely be related to this (Davidson, pp. 144-148).

Odin is also associated with ecstasy, possession, and mediation between living and dead. Davidson notes:

> The picture of the god as the bringer of ecstasy is in keeping with the most acceptable interpretation of the Germanic name Wodan, that which relates it to *wut* meaning high mental excitement, fury, intoxication, or possession. The Old Norse adjective *odr*, from which *odinn*, the later form of his name in Scandinavia, must be derived, bears a similar meaning: "raging, furious, intoxicated," and can be used to signify poetic genius and inspiration. Such meanings are most appropriate for the name of a god who not only inspired the battle fury of the berserks, but also obtained the mead of inspiration for the Aesir, and is associated with the ecstatic trance of the seer. (p. 147)

In ancient and contemporary shamanism, the sorcerer, in his ecstatic state, is believed to course through the air across the universe on a mount of bird or horse as did Odin on his eight-legged Sleipnir.

Now the question of whether the Mari is image, totem, sacrificed beast, priest or deity would be moot if we viewed her in the context of these primitive religious impulses. In magico-religious theory the thing and the image are inseparable; what represents a thing is in fact that thing. A beast sacrificed to a god becomes that god, and drinking the blood, eating the flesh and donning hide and skull of the sacrificed animal brings the celebrant into union with the god. Moreover, as Hays points out, in his ritual trance the shaman becomes the god, identifying "in true totemic relationship" with the animal-deity, until the latter subjugates the shaman (p. 158). More will be said later about the shamanistic traits of frenzy and shape-shifting as they concern poetic inspiration.

In making this comparison with Odin, we need not be too much concerned that the Mari of recent custom and of Watkins's Ballad is feminine. In matters smacking of shamanism, sexual confusion and interchange is unremarkable. Among present-day Siberian shamans, as Hays notes:

> Certain men change their sex and are considered to be the most powerful shamans of all. This inversion runs from mild transvestism . . . to real inversion. . . . On the mythical plane there is even belief . . . that his organs finally turn into those of a woman. (p. 416)

This tidbit is also interesting: the shaman of the Yakut tribe "lies on a white mare's skin . . . then puts on his magician's coat which may be a female garment or be painted with symbolic breasts" (p. 156).

Accounts of priests dressed like women recur in descriptions of ancient and modern shamanistic rites. Tacitus tells of priests "decked out like women" (*muliebris ornatus*) worshipping horsemen gods called the Alcis in forest sanctuaries (Davidson, p. 169). One is reminded of the self-emasculation of the frenzied priests of the androgynous Cybele,[4] and the effeminacies of the priests of the Norse twin deities Freyr and Freyja associated with horse sacrifice (Davidson, p. 97). Davidson also notes: "Men dressed as women and the use of clapping bells have survived into our own time in the annual mumming plays and dances which go with them" (p. 97), and we remember among the morris dancers in hobby-horse ceremonies, Mollie (a diminutive of Mary), the grotesquely dressed "man-dame" sweeping the earth with a broom in various Hooden Horse accounts. Then there is "Megan, the hag of the night," usually a male in female dress, described by Marie Trevelyan as accompanying the morris dancers in Welsh ceremonies, somewhat reminiscent of "Mallt-y-Nos, or Matilda of the Night," crying aloud when Arawn hunts with the Cŵn Annwn (pp. 30, 49-50).

There is also the possibility of the sexual confusion having occurred etymologically. The name Mari, which automatically

4 See E. O. James, *The Cult of the Mother Goddess*, pp. 167-168.

suggests "Mary" or "Marie," may not have been a proper name at all, especially when we consider that the Welsh name for Mary is not Mari, but Mair. Provoking speculation that the Mari Lwyd may originally have been a stallion is the fact that the Welsh for stallion or horse is *march* (Irish *marc*) from the inferred Indo-European base **marko*, seen now only in Celtic. As a masculine noun, *march* would have taken the base form of the adjective, *Llwyd*—instead of *lwyd*—a form sometimes appearing in the spelling of the custom. It is interesting to conjecture whether the proximity of the Welsh sounds *ch* and *ll* might not have caused the corruption of *march llwyd* (grey horse) into Mari Lwyd, with the subsequent "correction" of the adjective to lenated form, and the capitalization of both words into a proper name. That the English form of the female horse is "mare" (out of Anglo-Saxon *mere* or *miere,* feminine of *mearh,* horse, akin to German *mahre,* jade) may have consolidated this corruption, as did all the other factors we shall discuss below.

In any event, evidence of sexual fluidity in the Odin legend exists in the feminine Wild Huntsman which crops up in Continental lore, as described here by Hays:

> In Mechlenburg it is a goddess who is said to lead the Wild Hunt. She is known as Frau Gode or Wode, the female form of Wuton or Odin. She rides a white horse on these occasions, and her attendants take the shape of hounds and all manner of wild beasts   (p. 53).

Supernatural Women Associated with Horses in Celtic Tradition

But there are other avenues to explore for sources both of the Mari of Custom, and Watkins's conception of her. Have hypothesized multiple sources for the Retinue of the Dead, and having glimpsed the syncretizing nature of Watkins's imagination, we are probably safe in assuming a complex and hybrid genealogy for the Mari beyond the permutations of the myths of Odin and Arawn.

The most obvious area for scrutiny is the persistent tradition in Celtic myth and lore of horse-associated females with more or less supernatural powers, a tradition with which Watkins was undoubtedly familiar.

Evidence of such a tradition has been found by various scholars in the ancient Irish and Welsh texts, in the Continental Arthurian Romances, in Welsh, Irish and Breton folklore and customs recorded over the last few centuries, and in Celtic inscriptions, dedications and other archaeological discoveries.

Traces of this tradition occur in the Four Branches of *The Mabinogion*. In the second episode of the First Branch, we read of a queen with supernatural attributes associated with horses. After Pwyll returns from Annwn, and is holding court at Arbeth, he mounts Gorsedd Arbeth, a magic mound, and sees "a lady on a big fine pale white horse" passing the mound at an easy-going pace.[5] Several attempts to overtake her, by courtiers and Pwyll himself, even on the fleetest horses, prove unsuccessful, though "her pace was no greater than before." When, finally, Pwyll speaks to her, begging her to stay, the maiden, Rhiannon, surprisingly acquiesces readily, offering herself as a bride to Pwyll.

Later in the story, when they are finally married and she gives birth, the baby is snatched away while the negligent ladies-in-waiting have fallen asleep. To cover themselves, they implicate Rhiannon (by inference) in a charge of child-eating by smearing her with blood and casting bones before her. Her unjust penance is "to sit every day near a horse-block that was outside the gate . . .and to offer guest and stranger to carry him on her back to the court"—in brief, to serve as a horse (p. 18).

Meanwhile, "Teyron Twryf Liant was lord of Gwent Is-Coed, and the best man in the world was he. And in his house there was a mare, and throughout his kingdom there was neither horse nor mare more handsome than she. And every May-eve she foaled, but no one knew one word concerning her colt." Teyrnon decided to keep watch this one May-eve night, and "At the beginning of the night the mare cast a colt, large, handsome, and standing up on the spot. Teyrnon rose up and remarked the sturdiness of the colt and as he was thus he heard a great commotion, and after the commotion, lo, a great claw through a window of the house and seizing the colt by the

5 Trans. Jones and Jones, pp. 10ff. (The quotations in the remainder of this account are from the same translation, pp. 18-21).

mane." Teyrnon saves the colt by cutting off the monster arm, and when he returns from useless pursuit of it, "at the door, lo, an infant boy in swaddling-clothes, with a sheet of brocaded silk wrapped around him. He took up the boy, and lo, the boy was strong for the age that was his."

They raise the boy to be a healthy youngster, who at four years "would bargain with the grooms of the horses to let him take them to water," whereupon Teyrnon's wife asks her husband to break the colt saved on the night the boy was found, and give it to the boy. Later the boy is recognized as the son of Pwyll and Rhiannon and restored to his parents.

In the Third Branch, Rhiannon is further associated with horses. In Lwyd's magic fortress she is said to have suffered the servitude of having "the collars of assess, after they had been carrying hay, about her neck" (p. 54). That she is twice put in the role of a horse suggests a myth-degrading process at work.

Suggestions of a goddess associated with horses are also to be found in the ancient Irish tales. First let us note the parallel between the birth of Pryderi (Rhiannon's son) and that of Cuchulainn, born of Dechtere at the same time as a mare is foaling. Twin foals are given to the child—one horse being the significant "Grey of Macha."[6]

And who is Macha? She is one of a trio of supernatural women called the Morrigan or Morrigna, having the power, in Irish tales, to shift shape, especially into crow or raven, and to influence the outcome of battle.[7] Among ten preliminary tales in the book of Leinster, there is one which tells of Macha appearing in the house of an Ulster farmer, making herself his wife and bringing him great wealth. One day, when, against her wishes, her husband sets out for feasting and horse-racing, she warns him not to speak of her or she would have to leave him. When the king's two horses win race after race, the farmer breaks the taboo by boasting that his wife can beat the swiftest horse in the realm. The king commands that Macha be brought,

6 See Anne Ross, *Pagan Celtic Britain* (London, 1967), p. 326. Parenthetical references to Ross in the text are to this work. For a discussion of the parallelism, see Kenneth Hurlstone Jackson, pp. 91-95.

7 See Loomis, p. 117; Graves, p. 370.

and when she pleads that she is close on her time, he forces her to run by threatening to kill her husband. She races and outruns the king's horses,[8] only to give birth to twins at the goal, at the same time cursing the Ulster people (Rees and Rees, p. 58). Queen Medb, "Drunk Woman"—perhaps to induce shamanistic frenzy—was another supernatural Irish woman who could outrun the swiftest horse.

The archeological evidence for a cult of a mare-goddess is even stronger than that of the ancient texts. The worship of a mare-goddess Epona ("Divine Horse") is revealed in dedications all over Europe. Ross calls her the most important horse deity in Gaul, and believes that though her cult may not have been introduced into Britain until Roman times, "it no doubt fused with the cult of such insular equivalents as Rhiannon and Macha" (p. 322). Epona was born of a mare and is regularly represented in iconography as mounted on a steed, sidesaddle, sometimes accompanied by foals. Ross comments:

> The great Celtic horse, cut into the chalk at Uffington, Berkshire, in close proximity to an Iron Age stronghold, and dating probably to the first century B.C. may portray the goddess in zoomorphic form. This cannot, however, be demonstrated, but the cult import of the hill drawing is not in question. The supposition that it may be connected with the cult of a goddess of the type of the Gaulish Epona, if not of this deity herself, is strengthened by the fact that the Irish hill known as Emain Macha, clearly a sacred site from the Bronze Age times, although not adorned with an equine portrait, is named after the goddess Macha, connected with horses. (pp. 322-324)

Rees and Rees point out that Epona, "sometimes styled Regina," was thought to have been concerned "as much with the journey of the soul after death as with the welfare of horses and mules and their attendants" (pp. 45-46).

Epona often appears to merge identity with Matrona, a Celtic river-goddess "widely worshipped from Cisalpine Gaul to the Rhone," Loomis says, who gave her name to the Marne

8 There is an interesting parallel of this episode in the Taliesin story. Taliesin bids Elphin wager the king that his horse can run swifter than the king's. Elphin's horse wins the race at a place "which at this day is called Morfa Rhiannedd." (Trans. Lady Charlotte Guest, p. 281).

and other rivers in Gaul (pp. 119 and 129). As her name denotes, this goddess was associated with maternity, fertility and the home. She was often represented as a triad called the Matronae or Matres ("mothers"), this triple nature identifying her with the Macha-Morrigan. Ross notes (p. 322) that Epona, too, in at least one dedication, is commemorated plurally as *Eponabus*. Matrona appears in insular mythology as Modron, "Mother," mother of the Welsh Mabon, "Sons." Modron is mentioned only briefly in "Culhwch and Olwen," one of the eleven tales of *The Mabinogion,* but Loomis links her with the Macha-Morrigan through a sixteenth-century manuscript (pp. 98 and 119).

The tradition of the Celtic horse-goddess continued into the Middle Ages, as Alexander MacBain, writing in 1883, observed. He claimed that the name Morrigan "is doubtless the same as that of Morgan le Fay,[9] and Lucy Allen Paton and R. S. Loomis have traced this connection, showing that the motif of extraordinary horses, the gift of extraordinary women, recurs often in Arthurian romance.[10] In Chretien's *Chevalier de la Charrette* Lancelot is given marvellous horses by both the wife and sister of Melagant, "prince of the realm from which no stranger returns." In *Historia Meriadoci,* a damsel abducted by the king of the land whence no one returns, gives Meriadoc a steed of marvellous beauty and strength. In the Welsh *Peredur,* one of the nine witches of Caer Loyw gives Peredur his choice of horse and arms, as it was fated she should. In Ulrich von Zatzikhoven's *Lanzelet,* the faery queen, the Lady of the Sea, gives her foster-son his fleet, strong, spirited steed with which he slays Iweret in his eternally green wood. In addition to being strong and swift, the steed given to Lancelot

9 *Celtic Mythology and Religion* (Stirling, 1917), p. 127.
10 Lucy Allen Paton, *Studies in the Fairy Mythology of Arthurian Romance* (New York, 1903, 1960), pp. 11-12, 148-150, and throughout. The two essays, "Morgan La Fée and the Celtic Goddesses," and "The Combat at the Ford in the *Didot Perceval,"* pp. 105-130 and 91-104, respectively, reprinted in *Wales and the Arthurian Legend,* contain Loomis's interesting argument. All the examples used are culled by Loomis, where precise references to the pertinent texts may be found.

by the fay La Dame du Lac in the *Vulgate Lancelot* is also white. In the Breton lais, Graelent is made the gift of "un destrier tot blanc" by his faery mistress, and in the English *Sir Launfal,* the gift of the faery lady is named Blaunchard because it is as "whyt as flour." The colour white being symbolic of supernatural light in traditional symbology (as in Watkins's own language of symbols, as we have seen) may explain the predominance of this colour in descriptions of magical and sacred steeds.

Loomis shows very precise connections between the mistress of Launfal and the Irish Macha, thereby establishing a continuous tradition from ancient Celtic myth to Romance:

> Remarkable are the resemblances between Launfal's mistress and Macha. Macha's watery origin is suggested by the fact that she is daughter of Strangeness, son of Ocean. Like the fay of Avalon, she offers herself to a human lover and is accepted. As with Launfal, his wealth at once increases. As with Launfal, she imposes on him a taboo "not to speak of her in the assembly." He breaks the taboo and boasts of her swiftness, as Launfal boasts of his mistress's beauty. Even more astonishing are the similiarities between the steeds of the fays and the Grey of Macha, Cuchulainn's horse. This steed came out of a lake, as presumably did the white steed of the Dame du Lac which she gave to Launcelot. The name, Grey of Macha, "implies that he had been sent from Macha's fairy abode as a gift to her mortal protégé." It was seemingly her own horse, just as Blaunchard was referred to by the fay as "my stede lel." (pp. 116-117)

The tradition of the Celtic equine goddess has survived, indeed, all the way into present-day fairy lore. J. A. MacCulloch connects the Matrona, the Matres and the Welsh Modron to twentieth-century fairies,[11] who in Wales are sometimes called *Y Mamau,* the mothers, and in Brittany "nos Bonnes Mères les Fées," our good mothers the fairies.[12] Loomis likewise completes his chain by connecting Morgen, Morgain La Fée, and various unnamed other fays of Arthurian romances, including Ladies of the Sea, and of the Lake, whether single or in triads or enneads, with Welsh and Breton fairies, especially with a Welsh nineteenth-century water sprite called Morgan, and a modern Breton Fairy called Marie (or Mari) Morgan about whom

11 *The Religion of the Ancient Celts* (Edinburgh, 1911), pp. 45 ff.
12 W. Y. Evans-Wentz, pp. 153, 203.

Evans-Wentz gives the following account—worthy of full quotation for the provocative associations it has with Watkins's Mari and the Retinue of the Dead:

> The *Morgan* is a fairy eternally young, a virgin seductress whose passion, never satisfied, drives her to despair. Her place of abode is beneath the sea; there she possesses marvellous palaces where gold and diamonds glimmer. Accompanied by other fairies, of whom she is in some respects the queen, she rises to the surface of the waters in the splendour of her unveiled beauty. By day she slumbers amid the coolness of grottoes, and woe to him who troubles her sleep. By night she lets herself be lulled by the waves in the neighbourhood of the rocks. The sea-foam crystallizes at her touch into precious stones, of whiteness as dazzling as that of her body. By moonlight she moans as she combs her fair hair with a comb of fine gold, and she sings in a harmonious voice a plaintive melody whose charm is irresistible. The sailor who listens to it feels himself drawn toward her, without power to break the charm which drags him onward to his destruction; the bark is broken upon the reefs; the man is in the sea, and the Morgan utters a cry of joy. But the arms of the fairy clasp only a corpse; for at her touch men die, and it is this which causes the despair of the amorous and inviolate Morgan. She being pagan, it suffices to have been touched by her in order to suffer the saddest fate which can be reserved to a Christian. The unfortunate one whom she had clasped is condemned to wander for ever in the trough of the waters, his eyes wide open, the mark of baptism effaced from his forehead. Never will his poor remains know the sweetness of reposing in holy ground, never will he have a tomb where his kindred might come to pray and weep. (pp. 200-201)

Is it possible Watkins's Living have reference to this terrifying, pagan horror story when they speak repeatedly of "the drowned and drunken eyes" of the Retinue of the Dead, and try to drive them "back to the seawave's fall"?

Loomis cautions against imputing any etymological relationship to Macha, Morrigan, Modron, Morgan—names "so tantalizingly similar and yet so bafflingly impossible to derive, one from another, by any phonetic or common-sense agency" (p. 124), so we should be even more wary of linking the Mari Lwyd by the superficial similarity of her name, either to the ladies of myth and romance, or to fairies like the Breton Mari Morgan. Still our quest is not one of scholarly fact; we are trying to reconstruct the enormously rich and complex "ground" of the poet's imagination, his intellectual bag of facts, pseudo-facts, impressions, memories, experiences, references, et cetera, on which his imagination must have worked in whatever quixotic way it would. Though no claim can be made that there is any certain connection of the Mari of tradition, or the Mari of Watkins's poem, with the long line of equine or equestrian and supernatural ladies outlined above, it can only deepen our experience of the poem to know, and to test Watkins's Mari against, this venerable genealogy.

The Great Goddess

Our enquiry into sources of the Mari cannot end with these Celtic ladies. Despite the multiplicity of names, their common characteristics bespeak a common origin. Moreover, the correspondences we have noted between Celtic and Norse myth concerning the shamanistic horse cult suggest a widespread community of cult ideas, as does evidence found in present-day folklore and custom of many countries (Hays, p. 115).

Who was the deity celebrated and propitiated and called up by the rites of this ubiquitous cult? The derivations of the names of the Celtic women are instructive:

> Teyrnon (*Tigernonos) really is the Great King, and Rhiannon (*Rigantona) the Great Queen who is to be equated with Modron (Matrona), the Great Mother, the father and mother respectively of Mabon (Maponos) the Great Son, with whom Pryderi is identified or at least confused.[13]

Loomis calls Matrona "Divine Mother," Ross calls Maponos "Divine Son," and Rees and Rees note that Morrigan means either "Great Queen" or "Queen of Phantoms." Loomis believes that "the name Rhiannon contains the same Celtic root as does the second element in the name . . . Morrigan" (p. 102), and Rees and Rees say that Epona ("Divine Horse") was also called "Regina."

Watkins tells us in his note that the ancient custom of the Mari Lwyd is "traceable perhaps to the White Horse of Asia" (p. 90), indicating his awareness of the origin of the horse cult in the Indo-European steppe culture. The deity worshipped by

13 Introduction to *The Mabinogion,* trans. Jones and Jones, p. xv. Note that modern Welsh *Rhianedd* means "queen, lady, virgin."

the steppe tribes was the Earth Mother, variously called the Great Goddess, the Moon Goddess and the White Goddess.

Sibylle von Cles-Reden points out that it was around the worship of the Great Mother-Goddess that the cult of the dead (which has been touched on above) centered: "To the followers of this religion the dead in their stone chambers mystically re-generated and powerful as never before lived on in the bosom of the great earth mother and mistress of birth and death" (p. 11). Sibylle von Cles-Reden's investigation of the huge monoliths and tombs strung across Europe traces the path of what Hays calls "the megalithic missionaries" (p. 155), who disseminated the cult of the Great Mother from the Middle East through the Mediterranean and Central Europe, accounting, Graves argues, for the similarities between the early myths of the Hebrews, Greeks and Celts (p. 61).

It is to Graves, one of the Great Goddess's most devoted admirers, that we go for her description, imaginatively com-pounded out of his wide reading. He sees her as the main persona in the "single, infinitely variable Theme" of poetry, which Theme he summarizes as follows:

> The Theme, briefly, is the antique story, which falls into thirteen chapters and an epilogue, of the birth, life, death and resurrection of the God of the Waxing Year; the central chapters concern the God's losing battle with the God of the Waning Year for love of the capricious and all-powerful Threefold Goddess, their mother, bride and layer-out. The poet identifies himself with the God of the Waxing Year and his Muse with the Goddess; the rival is his blood-brother, his other self, his weird. All true poetry . . . celebrates some incident or scene in this very ancient story . . . (p. 24).

Elsewhere he expatiates on this complex relationship of mother/mistress/slayer and son/lover/victim:

> She [the Great Goddess] has a son who is also her lover and her victim, the Star-son, or Demon of the Waxing Year. He alter-nates in her favour with his tanist Python, the Serpent of Wisdom, the Demon of the Waning Year, his darker self. (p. 393)
> In Europe there were at first no male gods contemporary with the Goddess to challenge her prestige or power, but she had a lover who was alternatively the beneficent Serpent of Wisdom, and the beneficent Star of Life, her son . . . The Son . . . was reborn every year, grew up as the year advanced, destroyed the Serpent, and

won the Goddess's love. Her love destroyed him, but from his ashes was born another Serpent which, at Easter, laid the *glain* or red egg which she ate; so that the Son was reborn to her as a child once more. . . .

The most familiar icon of Aegean religion is therefore a Moon-woman, a Star-son and a wise spotted Serpent grouped under a fruit-tree—Artemis, Hercules and Erechtheus. Star-son and Serpent are at war; one succeeds the other in the Moon-woman's favour, as summer succeeds winter, and winter succeeds summer; as death succeeds birth and birth succeeds death. . . .

There are as yet no fathers, for the Serpent is no more the father of the Star-son than the Star-son is of the Serpent. They are twins. . . (pp. 387-388).

Graves has given us a vivid picture of the elemental Mother-Goddess:

The Goddess is a lovely, slender woman with a hooked nose, deathly pale face, lips red as rowan-berries, startingly blue eyes and long fair hair; she will suddenly transform herself into sow, mare, bitch, vixen, she-ass, weasel, serpent, owl, she-wolf, tigress, mermaid or loathsome hag. Her names and titles are innumerable. In ghost stories she often figures as "The White Lady," and in ancient religions, from the British Isles to the Caucasus as the White Goddess. . . . The reason why the hairs stand on end, the eyes water, the throat is constricted, the skin crawls and a shiver runs down the spine when one writes or reads a true poem is that a true poem is necessarily an invocation of the White Goddess, or Muse, the Mother of All Living, the ancient power of fright and lust—the female spider or the queen-bee whose embrace is death.

Sometimes, in reading a poem, the hairs will bristle at an apparently unpeopled and eventless scene described in it, if the elements bespeak her unseen presence clearly enough: for example, when owls hoot, the moon rides like a ship through scudding cloud, trees sway slowly together above a rushing waterfall, and a distant barking of dogs is heard; or when a peal of bells in frosty weather suddenly announces the birth of the New Year. (pp. 24-25)

It is this terror that Watkins's Ballad captures when he writes of the "sweat that springs in the hair" and the horror that makes "the knee-joints knock" (p. 71), as the dead retinue of the "White Spirit" "shudders free from the ground so white" (p. 71), to "tear through the frost of the ground" (p. 70), in the freezing cold at the joint of the years.

It is interesting to note here that the stark simplicity of the ballad form intensifies the usual electrifying, scalp-prickling substance of any ballad; the callous vengefulness of Barbara

Allan, followed by remorse (the very essence of the Theme or "antique story" Graves has outlined); patricide with the mother's collusion in "Edward"; murder by the true-love in "Lord Randal" (again the ancient theme); presentiment of and the subsequent death by drowning after the omen of the new moon with the old moon in her arms, in "Sir Patrick Spens"; the incarnation of the dead sons of the Wife of Usher's Well; and the corpse-picking horror of "The Twa Corbies" while the dead knight's lady goes off with another mate. The same clash of simple form and shocking substance operates in the literary ballads of the Romantic Movement which deal with the ancient Theme or the supernatural. Graves has treated at length Keats's "La Belle Dame Sans Merci" and Coleridge's "The Ancient Mariner" (pp. 427-435), and Watkins must have appreciated the same quality in Heine, whose work he admired and translated.[14]

Perhaps Watkins does not do as much justice as he might to the metaphysical levels in the old ballads in the following statement:

> My own ballads have a great deal in common with those of tradition. They are all rhythmical and intended to be read aloud; and in some I use a refrain. They are not in any sense private poems. Yet here the likeness ends. These ballads are elemental and they belong to myth, but they do not belong to history. In these it is not the narrative but the metaphysical situation that counts and the symbols surrounding the situation.[15]

The myth and symbols of the "ancient story" and the supernatural questions treated in many ballads would seem to give more of a metaphysical thrust to their literal, narrative levels than Watkins acknowledges, and would put him further into the ballad tradition than he recognized.

But let us return from this digression to Graves's introduction of the Great Goddess. Probing her ultimate origins, he goes back to the ancient religions of Sumer and Babylon to find:

> Belili, the Sumerian White Goddess, Ishtar's predecessor, who was a goddess of trees as well as a Moon-goddess, Love-goddess and Underworld-goddess. She was sister and lover to Du'uzu, or Tammuz, the Corn-god and Pomegranate-god. (p. 58)

14 See "To Heinrich Heine" in *Affinities*, p. 49.
15 "First Choice," *Poetry Book Society Bulletin, 1 (May, 1954), 1.* Quoted in *"Vernon Watkins",* Swansea *Evening Post*, May 13, 1954, p. 3.

Although her characteristics remain fairly constant, the goddess takes many names along the route of her dissemination, as, for example:

> Cotytto, or Cotys, who was worshipped orgiastically in Thrace, Corinth and Sicily. Her nocturnal orgies, the Cotyttia, were according to Strabo celebrated in much the same way as those of Demeter, the Barley-goddess of primitive Greece, and of Cybele, the Lion-and-Bee goddess of Phrygia in whose honour young men castrated themselves. (p. 62)

Among others, the Pelasgian Eurynome or Danae, the Greek Hera and Diana, Persephone, Aphrodite, Hekate, the White Cow Io, nurse of Dionysus, the White Mare Leucippe, who ultimately became the goddess Isis of Egypt, and Rahab in Jerusalem, are all variations of the same Great Goddess, Graves contends.[16]

We noted repeatedly the three-fold nature of the Celtic women discussed above (of the Morrigna, the Matres, the Eponabus), a characteristic which confirms their relationship to the Great Goddess. Over and over Graves emphasizes her multiple nature, referring to her often as the "Triple Goddess." We have seen that he calls her "mother, bride and layer-out," for she is a "personification of primitive woman—the creatress and destructress." Her "Whiteness" which partly symbolizes her divinity, also figures forth her ambivalence:

> In one sense it [white] is the pleasant whiteness of pearl-barley, or a woman's body, or milk, or unsmutched snow; in another it is the horrifying whiteness of a corpse, or a spectre, or leprosy. (p. 485)

In the discussion of whiteness above, we have seen how Watkins's imagination sustained the same paradox in the symbol, clearly working independently, since Watkins's "Ballad of the Mari Lwyd" and his "Music of Colours—White Blossom" were published before Graves wrote *The White Goddess*. Undoubtedly for both of them these symbolic connections were the product of wide and intimate acquaintance with the myths and rites of many traditions, and it would be interesting to discover each of their sources and to make a comparison between them.

16 E. O. James's valuable study, *The Cult of the Mother-Goddess*, covers the same ground.

On her creative side, the Great Goddess evinces further ambiguity. She has her reputable side associated with marriage, the family and the birth of children, and she has that side which Christian writers hint at with horror and loathing, associated with orgiastic fertility rites ending in the slaying of her brother-lover-son. Then there is the ambiguity of her destructive side, concerned with war and death. She destroys only to resurrect. All in all, she is maternal, sexual and lethal; but after she has created, mated with, and destroyed man she starts the cycle all over again.

Writing of her triple nature in various symbolic connections Graves notes:

> As Goddess of the Underworld she was concerned with Birth, Procreation and Death. As Goddess of the Earth she was concerned with the three seasons of Spring, Summer and Winter. As Goddess of the Sky she was the Moon in her three phases of New Moon, Full Moon and Waning Moon. . . . As the New Moon or Spring she was girl; as the Full Moon or Summer she was woman; as the Old Moon or Winter she was hag. (p. 386)

Although white was her principal colour, because, among other things, "the colour of the first member of her moon-trinity," other colours were symbolically associated with her different phases: "The New Moon is the white goddess of birth and growth; the Full Moon, the red goddess of love and battle; the Old Moon, the black goddess of death and divination" (p. 70). In her role of corn goddess, these colours were applied to her worship "in her triple capacity of white raiser, red reaper, and dark winnower of grain" (p. 70).

We shall return to this question of her triple nature when we come to discuss in the next chapter Watkins's description of his Mari, principally as defined by her Retinue of the Dead. But let us here complete Graves's description of his enormously complex and ubiquitous Great Mother, by showing how he connected the Great Mother in Greek myth with her Celtic emanations, some of whom we have already seen, through details of the horse cult. For example, there is a story about Rhea that when she gave birth to Poseidon, she offered her lover, Cronos, a foal to eat instead of the child, whom she gave secretly into the keeping of shepherds (p. 385). This interchange of foal and child, the separation of child and mother, and the suggestion of child-eating by the parent, occur, as we have seen in the story of Rhiannon in the First Branch of *The Mabinogion.*

Graves makes a further connection between Greek and Celtic myth through Demeter, clearly an emanation of the Great Goddess by virtue of her vital role in the seasonal myth, as well as through attributes that reveal her a Mare-goddess. She disguised herself as a mare to escape Poseidon's advances, and concealed herself among the horses of Oncios the Arcadian. That Poseidon became a stallion and covered her anyway is said to account for her statue at Onceum entitled Demeter the Fury (p. 384). Graves connects Demeter to the Celts through Epona, and thence to Rhiannon. The charge of child-eating (albeit trumped-up) against Rhiannon, connects her also with Leucippe (meaning "White Mare") who ran wild with her sisters and devoured her son Hippasus ("foal").

Sir James Frazer had made the essential connection between the Corn Goddess and the Mare Goddess in *The Golden Bough,* with which Watkins was undoubtedly intimately acquainted. Speaking of the Phigalian Demeter, Frazer comments:

> It was said that in her search for her daughter, Demeter assumed the form of a mare to escape the addresses of Poseidon, and that, offended at his importunity, she withdrew in dudgeon to a cave not far from Phigalia in the highlands of Western Arcadia. . . . There, robed in black, she tarried so long that the fruits of the earth were perishing, and mankind would have died of famine if Pan had not soothed the angry goddess and persuaded her to quit the cave. In memory of this event, the Phigalians set up an image of the Black Demeter in the cave; it represented a woman dressed in a long robe, with the head and mane of a horse.[17]

Although Frazer argues against viewing Demeter as the Earth Mother, and limits her role to Corn Goddess, he here observes that the Black Demeter is "plainly a mythical expression for the bare wintry earth stripped of its summer mantle of green." Frazer also recounts various harvest customs in England, Scotland and the Continent, which reveal the corn-

17 *The Spirits of the Corn and the Wild,* Part V of *The Golden Bough* (London, 1925) II, 21-22.

spirit to have been conceived of as a horse or mare. For
example, when the corn bends before the wind, the country
people believe the Corn-mother is present, and some say:
"There runs the Horse" (I, 292, 303). The first or last sheaves of
the harvest are given special significance, sometimes being
stored for feeding to a mare in foal on the first day of Christmas (I, 160), an event which is often followed by a sacramental
meal of barley and ale, which Frazer hypothesizes is the equivalent of the sacramental draught in the solemn rite of the Eleus-
inian mysteries (I, 161, n. 4). Does Watkins's refrain "Chalice
and Wafer, Wine and Bread," and the suggestions of the
Eucharist in the table spread with a white cloth loaded with
food and ale, have any affinities with the sacramental meal of
these corn spirit ceremonies? We shall consider this later.

In another part of this work Frazer discusses the annual rites
associated with Hippolytus (Greek hippos, a horse),
worshipped by the Romans as the God Virbius, "the first of the
divine Kings of the Wood at Aricia," in whose rites, Frazer sur-
mises, the horse was sacrificed not as a victim to propitiate the
god, but as a surrogate (11, 40-47). This Divine Foal was son of
Hippolyta (whose name suggests her kinship with the Mare-
Goddess), and victim of his "mother" Phaedra, probably a
further manifestation of the Great Goddess who seduces and
kills the Divine Son in this much debased telling of the myth of
the cycle of death and rebirth of the seasons. In the rites of the
Divine King Hippolytus/Virbius, Frazer notes, a ritual horse
race culminates in the severing of the head of the right-hand
horse which is adorned with a string of loaves—a detail which
links the rite to the rites of spirits of the corn. The parallel to the
horse races involving Macha and Taliesin mentioned above is
notable.

Adding further insights into the cult of the horse (and thus
deepening our "ground" for appreciation of Watkins's Ballad),
Frazer points to a modern primitive rite, quoting A. Play-
fair's account of a custom among the Garos in Assam:

> When the rice harvest has been fully gathered in, the great sacri-
> fice and festival of the year . . . takes place. . . . A curious feature of
> the ceremony is the manufacture of *gure* or "horses" out of pieces

of plantain-stem for the body, and of bamboo for the head and legs. The image of the "horse" is laid on the floor of the *nokma's* house, and the assembled guests dance and sing around it the whole night long, with the usual intervals for refreshments. Early the next morning, the "horse" is taken to the nearest river and launched on the water to find its way down stream on the current. For those who possess the necessary paraphernalia, the *gure* takes the shape of a horse's head of large size, made of straw, and covered with cloth. (II, 337-339)

A specific *gure* observed by the reporter is described as ornamented with discs of brass on both sides of the face, and eyes and ears of the same metal. Bronze bells were attached to the head. The account continues:

The manner in which this form of *gure* is used is the following. The head is mounted on a stick, which a man holds before him in such a way that the head comes up to the level of his chest. Two straps pass over his shoulders to relieve his hands of the weight. The body of the "horse" is then built round his own body with cane and cloth. The performer thus apparelled, commences to dance a shuffling step to the usual music. In front of him dances the priest, who goes through the pantomime of beckoning the animal to come to him. The remaining guests . . . form a *queue* behind the "horse," and dance after it.

When the festival is over, "the *gure* is taken to a stream and the body thrown into the water, the head being preserved for another year." A sacramental meal and rite follows comparable to those mentioned above. Frazer speculates:

If we knew more about the rites of the horse-headed Demeter at Phigalia, we might find that amongst them was a dance of a man or woman who wore the mask of a horse's head and personated the goddess herself, just as, if I am right, the man who dances disguised as a horse at the harvest festival of the Garos, represents the spirit of the rice dancing among the garnered sheaves.

Many details in this extended description are so evocative of the Mari Lwyd ceremony of tradition and of the Ballad that they need no comment.

Poems of Mare and Foal

Watkins deals with the nature of mare and foal in a number of poems throughout the canon, which reveal him to be at ease with, and in command of, the whole complex of myth surrounding the Mare-Mother-Goddess. This is to say that he wields no heavy or mechanical hand in mythic allusions. Resonances are not achieved by intrusion of direct reference to myth. On the contrary, one may read the words and seize the images as "merely descriptive of natural appearances," to use Kathleen Raine's words (p. 119). But "those who are familiar with the universal language of symbolic discourse," that "secret language," as she calls it, of traditional symbol and myth, will know at once that the images in Watkins's poem are also invested with other values. These values seem to derive from the cult of the Earth-Mare-Mother.

Let us take first the poem "Cornfields" (*Fidelities*, p. 48), which contains a number of lines about foal and mare. While we may appreciate the unity of life which the poem celebrates without knowledge of the Corn-and-Barley-and-Mare Goddess, Demeter-cum-Rhiannon, we shall, in the first place miss some important allusions, and secondly, experience a much shallower response, if we do not bring the teeming associations surrounding her to our reading. The poem begins straighforwardly enough, if we take it down to the middle of the second stanza, making its way with ease and clarity on the purely naturalistic level:

> Corn waves in the wind;
> A sigh, early and late.
> The eye of the barley is blind
> When the stalk is stiff and straight.
>
> Ears, ripening, rise,
> Then gold, heavily fall;

But what are we to make of the last two lines of the second stanza:

> The breath of nativity sighs:
> The star is laid in the stall.

Since we know that Watkins was a practising Christian, and since we live in a still predominantly Christian context, we may read these lines solely as a parallel of the corn's fruition to the birth in the stable's manger (stall) of Christ, the Star seen by the wise men and the shepherd in the fields—even though "star" is

81

not capitalized as we might expect. But is it over-reaching to suggest that Watkins may have had more in mind than the Christian story alone? Just as Frazer and Graves and others have observed the merging of pagan myth into Judeo-Christian beliefs, might not Watkins's syncretizing imagination have unified elements of the earlier seasonal myth of the birth, death and resurrection of the Star Son of the Great Mother with the Christian Star Son? Certainly in Watkins's vision, if not in the Christian story itself, the star laid in the stall carries the hint of a foal-child—the proper offspring for the Corn-and-Mare Goddess — since in the very next stanza Watkins speaks of "a foal unborn/To the mare asleep in the grass." The fact that foal and mare constantly exemplify the cycle of animal life, in comparison with the cycle of plant life, throughout the canon, may suggest more than a casual choice or a personal symbol.

In the myth of the Mare-cum-Corn Goddess and her Star Son, primitive man wrestled with the mysteries of his own nature, struggling to make sense of his human condition in terms of the seasonal development of plant life, in whose process of generation, growth and decay he could see hope of re-generation. In "Cornfields" Watkins wrestles with much the same question. In the cycle of the corn the poet sees the cycle of bird and beast, apprehending in the corn's vitality the foal hidden in the mare's belly, and the wings rustling, or about to rustle in the nest. In fact, in any given amount of the cycle of any particular growing thing, the poet apparently sees the whole cycle of each and all living things, and finally the unity of all life:

> Learn, learn of the corn
> Of things come to pass,
> Of wings, and a foal unborn
> To the mare asleep in the grass.

Similarly in the first stanza the barley's eye is conceived of as blind—like that of the newborn foal—in its early, unripe state, when the stalks stand straight, that is, when the stalks are not weighed down by the weight of the ripe grain.

Each living thing not only symbolizes the other, not only in a sense *is* the other; each natural entity, vegetable or animal, senses a community of being with the others:

> Crest follows on crest;
> A sigh moving in air,
> A rustling of wings in the nest
> Ascends from the dreaming mare.

In the last two stanzas, shaped in the form of a meditative question, the birth tremor is understood as a summons activating harvest as well as germination, indeed activating *all* of nature to take part in the seed's cycle:

> Birth's tremor within
> The fruit earth has concealed,
> Does it summon life to begin
> And the sun to reap the field,
>
> Joy weighing at dusk
> The scales, heavy and light,
> The balance of ear and husk,
> Daybreak dreaming of night?

The poet's vision engages the paradox that in any moment of the cycle of life there is past, present and future in a sense of eternal present-ness. He considers the miracle of all created things, of the constantly moving process of life to death, to re-birth, inherent in the birth tremor, or any other given instant. What man knows intellectually — that seed will become ear will become husk — the seed "knows" in that mysterious way that is like dreaming, where will plays no part, at least not the will of the dreamer. The mare dreams in this figurative way, as well as literally. Daybreak "dreams" in the sense that it is the inevitable beginning of a circle which contains its own inevitable end. The traditional symbol for this concept is the ouroboros, that circular serpent biting its own tail to symbolize self-fecundation and the cyclic pattern of self-sufficient nature. The fact that Watkins passed up this and other symbols perhaps manifests a preference for the implicit rather than the explicit use of myth and symbol, and explains why his poem works well eough to a reader for whom only the "naturalistic" level is available. But a full impact awaits the time that a reader arms himself with a context closer to that which the poet must have possessed at his writing of the poem. The ramifications of the myth of the Corn-

and-Mare Goddess, the Great Earth Mother, were surely part of that creative ground.

The "dreaming mare" is the focus of the poem "The Mare" *(Cypress and Acacia,* p. 24). Again, this poem may be enjoyed on a purely naturalistic level, as the description of a pregnant mare indolently lying down to sleep in the meadow while the lark sings and the wind blows gently over her, a scene which re-creates in the mind's eye the serenity of grazing horses on the Commons of the Gower Peninsula. Even on this level the poem wins its place as one of Watkins's most breathtaking pieces by virtue of the aura of delicacy, translucence and mystery which he has engendered. The miracle of pregnancy and maternity is conveyed by the terms in which the untroubled state of the mare's consciousness is conveyed. As her eyes rove "the delicate horizon," she begins to fall asleep, a sensation magically evoked by the poet's projection of her internal state outwards onto nature, in the description: "Deep sink the skies, a well of voices." The blissful, contented quality of the mare's slumber is conveyed by the image of her sleep as "a vessel of summer," and by the surrender of her body to the light of the heavens and the gentle wind:

> The mare lies down in the grass where the nest of
> the skylark is hidden.
> Her eyes drink the delicate horizon moving
> behind the song.
> Deep sink the skies, a well of voices. Her sleep
> is the vessel of Summer.
> That climbing music requires the hidden music at rest.
>
> Her body is utterly given to the light, surrendered
> in perfect abandon
> To the heaven above her shadow, still as her first-born
> day.
> Softly the wind runs over her. Circling the meadow,
> her hooves
> Rest in a race of daisies, halted where butterflies stand.

Again the moment (this moment that the poet freezes in the poem) recapitulates her entire life cycle—the sky is the same sky she "knew" the day she was born. Even as she sleeps, her hooves circle the meadow. Even as they circle, they are halted where butterflies, ever-fluttering, stand.

Again, these images do not only suggest the blissful repose of a particular mare. They also operate to express Watkins's awe at the miracle of all pregnancy. More than that, they celebrate the miracle of all generation, the miracle of the hidden, germinating seed lying in the secret dark (night dreaming of day), the miracle of time and season themselves, of "day dreaming of night," of spring summoning winter. The "hidden music at rest" describes not only the foal carried by the mare, but all life secretly awaiting regeneration. The naturalistic music, the "climbing music" of the lark soaring from his nest "requires" (in the sense of the unwilled, uncoercing necessity of nature that is akin to dreaming) the nadir to his zenith, music that is hidden and at rest, the other stages of the life cycle, and all of the cycle of life. For music, as we have seen in "Music of Colours—White Blossom," carries the symbolic value of transcendence, ideality, and the life force, which is love, which is light—which is light even when buried in secret darkness. In "Cornfields" the unity of nature is conveyed with the image of the mare dreaming of rustling wings; in "The Mare" the bird's song "requires" the beast's gravidity.

Necessity in the poem, however, is no inexorable force. Like the dream, this life stuff is delicate. A scales, a sensitive balance, are images Watkins sometimes uses, as in "Cornfields." Accident, clumsiness, man's perverted will, can disturb the balance, cut the thread, break the circle. The last stanza of "The Mare" is a reminder of the vulnerability of growing things:

> Do not pass her too close. It is easy to break the circle
> And lose that indolent fullness rounded under the ray
> Falling on light-eared grasses your footsteps must not yet wake.
> It is easy to darken the sun of her unborn foal at play.

The time in the life cycle for the birth of the foal is not yet ripe. The rounded belly of the mare and the life cycle are symbols of each other, both together vulnerable to violation if the foal is waked before his time, just as the grass, light-eared, that is, too young for falling, for reaping (that is, at the same stage as the blind-eyed barley in "Cornfield"), may have its life cycle broken by clumsy footsteps. The final line is a marvellous compression of present and future, the foal *in utero,* the foal born and at play; the sun that is to shine on him (as the ray is now shining on mare and grass) will be "darkened" for him before he has chance to see its light (as his mare-mother saw the light of the heaven on *her* first day) if the clumsy passer-by startles the mare, causing her to miscarry.

Now even with all these rich associations, we shall miss a complete reading of the poem unless we recognize a still further level operating in the poem. More than particular mare, generic mare, and mare symbolic of the total life principle, she is also mythic mare. "That indolent fullness rounded under the ray," the literal curve of her belly, is not just symbolically equated with the circle of life, the cycle of growth. It is like the earth, as an orb or as a round hill of the earth; it is *of* the earth, and indeed, it *is* the earth itself. In the myth of the Great Goddess, Mare Goddess and Earth Mother are inseparably identified. In the *Satapatha Brahmana* of Vedic literature, we find precisely this symbolic equation of earth and mare:

> 25. Thereupon, whilst touching her (the earth), "Thou art Manu's mare," for having become a mare, she (the earth) indeed carried Manu, and he is her lord, Pragapati: and with that mate his heart's delight, he thus supplies and completes him.[18]

No mechanical application of myth, no specific allusions, no pastiche of references of the kind to require an exhausting gloss and to create an obstruction in a "simple" reading of the poem, occur in this poem any more than in "Cornfields," so thoroughly integrated are all levels, so gracefully at ease is Watkins's imagination with the context and language of symbol and myth. The only way we can test that the myth of the great Goddess is fundamental to this poem, so little does Watkins draw our conscious attention to the fact, is by judging *after* the fact whether our knowledge of the myth enhances our appreciation, our "felt experience," of the work, without distorting our experience of the naturalistic level.

18 *The Sacred Books of the East,* Ed. F. Max Müller (Oxford, 1900), XVIV, 465.

In "Foal" (*The Lady with the Unicorn*, p. 43). the same images are at work, the foal and the mare, the fine-eared grass, and the bird (this time a starling), the earth, the sky and the air, on the descriptive level; and the circle, the vessel, darkness and light on the symbolic level. While once more Watkins celebrates the mystery of life, the emphasis shifts slightly, past the principle of maternity and the miracle of pre-birth and generation, to the miracle of vitality and the renewal of life as represented by the offspring, the newly-born foal.

Again the mere naturalistic detail of the newborn foal's delicacy and beauty generates lightness and radiance, and informs the poem with its own magic—the magic of "washed eyes." And again Watkins comes to grips with the metaphysical question of the perpetuation of life far beyond the transient life of this particular foal. He conveys simultaneously his vision of the individual, the general, and the ideal through an image of twin foals. The foal existing in nature, is a white or light foal—white here being not the colour of ideality, but natural white, the farthest extension of the warm, "advancing" colours of activity and intensity. His twin is a blue foal—blue, in colour symbolism, being associated with the "retreating" colours moving back towards passivity and darkness, towards black (Cirlot, p. 50). Watkins tells us, before introducing his light and dark twins:

> Darkness is not dark, nor sunlight the light of
>   the sun
> But a double journey of insistent silver hooves.

Darkness is not negatively conceived, and light is not just meant literally. As we have seen from the "Music of Colour" poems, darkness is the secrecy of becoming in which light is buried or hidden until it becomes being. Light is life, is love or the life force; it breaks within, and it breaks on, the natural foal as an illuminating flash, at the tremor of birth:

> Light wakes in the foal's blind eyes as lightning
>   illuminates corn
> With a rustle of fine-eared grass, where a starling
>   shivers.

Let us note in passing how again the unity of nature is conveyed by the simile of the quickening of corn and starling (the rustle, the shiver of the birth tremor) to describe the accession of light and life in the foal.

In the twin image then, dark and light are not viewed as antipathetic, but as complementary principles in the circle of life, comparable to the binary symbol of contrasting but interlocked "tadpole" shapes within a circle (created by the bissecting sigmoid line) of the Chinese Yang and Yin, the light side suggesting sun, heat, heaven, activity and "masculinity"; the dark side suggesting the soft, cold secrecy of the passive "feminine" principle of earth. Just as Yang and Yin are interlocked in a way to signify that each mode contains within it the germ of its antithesis, so in Watkins's poem light is potential or incipient in darkness, as darkness is in light.

Whenever a particular foal is born, circles the meadow, or stoops to suckle, there is not just one foal, the living foal of light, but the dark foal, "the vessel of ages/Clay-cold, blue." Who is this "left spirit, vanished, yet here?" It is both the foal now dead, or a coalescence of the chain of dead antecedents of the present foal, who once raced around the meadow as the new foal now races, and the foal yet to be born, whether brother or son of the presently living foal, or a quintessence of all foals yet to be born. "Left" may then have connotations of "gone," as implied by "vanished"; and of "left behind" in the vast repository, "the vessel of ages," out of which all life comes. The antithetical effect of "left" to right, as light to dark, may also reverberate here:

And whoever watches a foal sees two images,
Delicate, circling, born, the spirit with blind eyes leaping
And the left spirit, vanished, yet here, the vessel of ages
Clay-cold, blue, laid low by her great wide belly the hill.

See him break that circle, stooping to drink, to suck
His mother, vaulted with a beautiful hero's back
Arched under the singing mane,
Shaped to her shining, pricked into awareness
By the swinging dug, amazed by the movement of suns;

His blue fellow has run again down into grass,
And he slips from that mother to the boundless
        horizons of air,
Looking for that other, the foal no longer there.

The dark foal, then, which suggests both the ghost of the dead foal gone from the meadow, and the essence of a foal yet to be conceived or born, may be generalized as the principle of continuity of foalness, the generations of foals that have already been, the generations yet to be, continuing in perpetuity. The blue foal is also the Ideal foal, more Real than any individual emanation of essential foalness, which perhaps explains why Watkins makes him blue in his darkness, not black. For blue is not only "darkness made visible," it is the colour which is associated with the purest white; it is also the colour of sky and sea, both associated with creation, eternity and ideality (Cirlot, pp. 50-52).

That the poem is indeed about foalness, generic and/or Ideal seems to be corroborated by its title "Foal," the lack of article distinguishing it from "The Mare."

Just as there are two foals in the poem, there are two mothers. The particular, naturalistic mother is there, lying in the grass, suckling her newborn foal. But the mare of the dark foal is there, too, as the generic and Ideal mother, a composite of marehood, which Watkins has embraced in the mythic image of the mare-earth with "her great wide belly the hill." Through this mere hint of the myth of the Earth-Mother, the foal is again identified with the seed in the earth, and again the community of vegetable and animal worlds is implied. This is an important metaphysical truth for grasping the symbolic meaning of the dark foal: it is easier to conceive of the continuity of the thread of life and the unbroken circle in terms of the cycle of plants from seed through leaf, flower and fruit, back to germinating seed in the dark earth, than it is to understand the perpetuation of man and beast, in natural as opposed to theological terms, beyond the obstacle of death. The most universal symbol for the renewal of life must be the earth herself. This earth is a pitcher, a vase, dark and full of music, in short a secret container of the life stuff, which is music, light and love, hidden and waiting to surge forth.[19] In the belly of this hill, this earth, "there is always a little foal/Asleep."

> But perhaps
> In the darkness under the tufted thyme and
>   downtrodden winds,
> In the darkness under the violet's roots, in the darkness
>   of the pitcher's music,
> In the uttermost darkness of a vase
> There is still the print of fingers, the shadow of waters.
> And under the dry, curled parchment of the soil
>   there is always a little foal
> Asleep.

Without making too much of it, we might add to our ambience for reading this poem knowledge of the double nature of the Star Son, who, as God of the Waxing Year dominates the cycle of growth up to the summer solstice when he is ritually murdered and succeeded by his twin, his blood brother, his tanist, his darker other self, his weird, his rival, the God of the Waning Year, as Graves variously calls him (pp. 24, 124-127, 357, 387-388, 393), who, in turn, is ritually murdered at the winter solstice, when the original twin-tanist is resurrected to start the cycle of life over again. It is certainly provocative to remember the implications of tanist-twinship with foals of the hero-sons of Celtic Mare-Mothers: Rhiannon's son Pryderi and the May-eve foal born the same night; Cuchulainn's birth at the same time as twin foals; Macha's twins born at the goal of the horse race. Perhaps Leda's twins, the Dioscuri, said to live half their lives on earth and half in heaven, were also revolving in Watkins's imaginative field as he wrote this poem.

It is not contended that this mythic material was applied in any of the mare-and-foal poems in a deliberate way—or even consciously for that matter. But it is surely there in the poetic ground. Can those who view Watkins as an orthodoxly Christian poet believe that he did not penetrate deeply into the

---

19 For the symbolic equations of cavern-matrix, see Mircea Eliade, *The Forge and the Crucible,* trans. Stephen Corrin (London, 1962), pp. 40 ff.; the matrix or uterus as a vase, p. 154, where Dorn, "Physica Trismegisti," 430, is quoted: "The vase is akin to the work of God in the vase of divine germination." Quoted by Jung, *Psychologie und Alchemis,* p. 325, n.i.

origins of the Mari when his imagination first seized upon her at such an early and critical stage in his poetic development? Graves said: "I am not a Welshman . . . but my profession is poetry, and I agree with the Welsh minstrels that the poet's first enrichment is a knowledge and understanding of myths" (p. 30). No one had to tell Watkins this. He must have known it in his marrow.

CHAPTER V

OTHER ATTRIBUTES OF WATKINS'S MARI, INCLUDING CONFLICTING CLAIMS OF THE LIVING AND THE DEAD

Perhaps the myth of the Great Goddess will also elucidate the other-than-equine attributes of the Mari listed in the first line of the Prologue: "Mari Lwyd, Horse of Frost, Star-horse, and White Horse of the Sea." These attributes are reinforced by the Dead claiming that frost, stars and sea are the source of their wit, since elsewhere they state that their source is the Mari.

The first thing to note is the trinity of these attributes which accord the Mari sway over the three realms of nature—earth, sky and sea. These are the three realms into which ancient cultures such as the Babylonian divided their universe. This trinity of roles seems to link the Mari with the Triple Goddess as much as does her equine nature.

As we have already noted, Graves has shown us that with the dissemination of the myth of the Great Mother she was given many names, emphasis being placed on different attributes from place to place. In many of her manifestations she is associated with the wintry earth and the starry sky. One of these, the Roman Goddess Cardea, whose name, Graves contends, means "hinge," was associated with the two-headed god Janus, and addressed by her celebrants as "Postvorta and Antevorta—she who looks both back and forward" (pp. 178-179), with power to "open what is shut; to shut what is open" (p. 69). Graves also states that this Goddess of Hinges was director of the four main winds, the *most* cardinal of which was Boreas, the North Wind: "She ruled over the Celestial Hinge at the Back of the North

Wind around which . . . the mill-stone of the Universe revolves."
Graves also claims that the giantesses in the Norse *Edda* "who
turn the monstrous mill-stone Grotte in the cold polar night,
also stand for the White Goddess in her complementary moods
of creation and destruction" (p. 178).

Besides the wintry and celestial associations, these aspects of
the Great Goddess would also seem to have particular relevance to Watkins's Mari, since she, too, governs the hinge of the
year. Watkins's play on the pivot of the pin of the tongs, that the
Living use to put coal on the fire, and the pin that "goes in to the
inmost dark/Where the dead and living meet" (p. 80), appears
to reinforce these associations.

According to Graves, "the Great She-bear and the Little She-
bear," the constellations Ursa Major and Ursa Minor, are said
to turn the mill around on its axis, the Little Bear pivoting on
the Pole-star. In our discussion of the Celtic Otherworld above,
the Great Bear's association with the "Peerless Land" of Thule,
in all its polar whiteness, has been noted, together with this
constellation's widespread characterization in many mythologies as a vehicle of the dead, explaining the claim of
Watkins's Dead that they have pulled "the Plough, . . . the Dead
Man's wain," out of the night.

Some mythographers identify the Great Goddess who lives at
the axis of the mill, whirling around without motion, as Rhea,
mother of Zeus, Queen of the Universe, one of the most elemental of the Great Mother's manifestations. Rhea is also
associated with the Milky Way. In fact, the Galaxy is said to
have been formed when her milk spurted across the sky at
Zeus's birth. The same story attached to Hera, who spattered
the sky with milk when Heracles bit her breast. The Galaxy is
also the "Path of Ghosts" over which the Valkyries led their
retinue of slain heroes, and over which Odin rode his grey steed,
Sleipnir to greet the fallen (Graves, pp. 85, 179).

There are other constellations besides the Plough and the
Milky Way associated with the Earth Mother or Triple
Goddess. Graves compellingly connects Cardea to the Welsh
Arianrhod, who appears in the Fourth Branch of *The Mabin-
ogi* as the mother of Llew Llaw Gyffes, identified by Graves

as an aspect of the Solar Hero or Star Son. It is to Arianrhod's castle that the dead are said to repair awaiting resurrection, this castle being a constellation named in Welsh star-lore after Arianrhod, and comprising one of the locations, according to Graves, of the Otherworld "House of Glass."

> . . . Arianrhod is one more aspect of . . . the White Goddess of Life-in-Death and Death-in-Life; and to be in the Castle of Arianrhod is to be in a royal purgatory awaiting resurrection. For in primitive European belief it was only kings, chieftains and poets, or magicians, who were privileged to be reborn. Countless other less distinguished souls wandered disconsolately in the icy grounds of the Castle . . . Where was this purgatory situated? . . . Well, where should one expect to find it? In a quarter from which the Sun never shines. Where is that? In the cold North. How far to the North? Beyond the source of Boreas, the North Wind; for "at the back of the North Wind"—a phrase used by Pindar to locate the land of the Hyperboreans—is still a popular Gaelic synonym for the Land of Death. But precisely where beyond the source of the North Wind3 . . . Caer Arianrhod (not the submerged town off the coast of Caernarvon but the real Caer Arianrhod) is, according to Dr. Owen of the *Welsh Dictionary,* the constellation called "Corona Borealis." Not *Corona Septentrionalis,* "The Northern Crown," but *Corona Borealis,* "The Crown of the North Wind." Perhaps we have the answer here to the question which puzzled Herodotus: "Who are the Hyperboreans3" Were the Hyperboreans, the "back-of-the-North-Wind-men", members of a North Wind cult, as the Thracians of the Sea of Marmara were? Did they believe that when they died their souls were taken off by Hermes, conductor of souls, to the calm silvered-circled castle at the back of the North Wind, of which the bright star Alpheta was the guardian? (pp. 98-99)

It is to this prison in the cold polar north from which the wind brings snow, and where "only dead suns are to be found," that the Sun-king (the Star-son) returns at death to the bosom of the White Moon Goddess.

In the 107th Triad Arianrhod is called the "silver-circled daughter of Don," and in his *Celtic Mythology and Religion,* p. 90, MacBain tells us that the whole family of Don "is connected with the sky and its changes." Don's daughter, Arianrhod, " 'silver-circled,' inhabits the bright circle of stars which is called the Northern Crown."

Graves claims that the Welsh heroines Blodeuwedd and Olwen are also attenuations of the Great Goddess, associated through the white track of the Milky Way with Rhea. It is possible that Watkins had the sky-prison room of glass of Caer Arianrhod and the White Track of Blodeuwedd and Olwen in mind when he described the Mari as:

> A stiff, star-struck thing
> Blown by the stinging spray
> And the stinging light of the stars,
> Our white, stiff thing,
> Death and breath of the frost,
> That has known the room of glass,
> Dropped by the Milky Way. . . .   (p. 77).

Most emanations of the Great Goddess have been entitled "Queen of Heaven," either by virtue of her association with the moon, or with the stars, in her more ancient manifestations. The Sumerian White Goddess was a goddess of the planet Venus. As the morning star she was Innana, goddess of war; as the evening star, Nana, the goddess of love and motherhood.[1] Innana was the precursor of the Akkadian star-goddess Ishtar, great goddess of Babylon, Assur and Mari, and numbers of other excavated cities in the Near East, whose diggings have revealed her eight-pointed symbol, the Star of Venus, the morning and evening star (Zehren, p. 79). In Egyptian myth the Goddess Nut, celestial counterpart of Nun (Chaos), was "Lady of Heaven" as well as "Mistress of Two Lands" on earth and proprietress of the dead in the underworld. Each day the Sun enters her in the Western Sky, impregnates her, and is reborn of her. Like Isis, says E. O. James, (pp. 58-59), "she was depicted usually with cow's horns and often in the form of a great cow with stars on her body and her legs corresponding to the four pillars at the cardial points of the compass. The stars were her children while the souls of the dead could be seen at night on her body as stars."

The Mari's final attribute in the important first line of the prologue of the Ballad, her being of the sea, needs hardly more explanation than a summary of points already made. If we glance back over the catalogue of women in Welsh myth and

---

1 Erich Zehren, *The Crescent and the Bull,* trans. James Cleugh (New York, 1962), p. 104.

legend associated with horses and the Otherworld, we discover a marked association with water. The Macha-Morrigan's association is with fords—as the ford where Cuchulainn fights Loch. Matrona, Loomis points out, was a water-divinity, giving her name to the Marne and other European rivers, and the composite Arthurian Morgain-and-other-fays was "a sort of naiad or nereid, haunting springs, rivers, fords, lakes and seas, or dwelling beneath their surface" (p. 128). Fairies of recent and modern lore more often than not come out of lake or sea, and many are virtually mermaids, as in the case of the Mari-Morgan of Brittany.[2]

Discussion above of the recurrent motif of an island as the location of the Otherworld, in Celtic myth and lore, suggests another reason for the Mari's association with the sea. Markings resembling ships found on tomb's and megaliths in Ireland, Britain, Brittany and in the Scandinavian countries, comparable to those in the sepulchral art of Egypt, suggest the journey across water of the soul after death, as do classical and present-day accounts of the Breton "ghost boat" which ferries the departed to the Island of the Dead, and the barge in Arthurian Romance which transports the dead king to Avalon, across the mere. Ocean and lake were apparently interchangeable in this Otherworld mythology. Strabo tells us, on the authority of Posidonius, of the sacred significance of lakes. He claims that vast votive treasures were submerged in many watery sanctuaries in *Celtica,* and the hoard recovered from Llyn Cerrig Bach in Anglesey in 1943 seems to bear him out.[3] Of the sacred spring as the source of inspiration, I shall have occasion to speak below.

It is interesting to note that the sea features in several of the British horsehead rites. Howey describes how, in a May Day rite still enacted at Padstow, Cornwall, the hobby-horse is

2 For an extended study of the mermaid and her antecedents, see Gwen Benwell and Arthur Waugh, *Sea Enchantress* (London, 1961), especially pp. 141 and 150 for references to the Morgan, which, the authors contend, means "born of the sea."

3 Strabo IV. i. 13. See Myles Dillon and Nora Chadwick, *The Celtic Realms* (New York, 1967), p. 137. References in the text to Dillon and Chadwick are to this work.

ridden into the waves and submerged after completing the circuit of the town (p. 84). We have already noted above that in Frazer's account of the *gure* ceremony in Assam, the horse effigy is taken to a stream and the body thrown into the water. This is a fate that the Living in Watkins's Ballad would wish on the Mari, telling her Retinue:

> Cast your Lwyd to the white spray's crest
> That pounds and rides the air.   (p. 75)

Loomis's description of the Arthurian fay as a "nereid" is more than apt because the connection between sea and horses goes back at least to the myth of Poseidon, god of sea and horses. Usually represented as having the body of a fish and the head of a horse, he was attended by the daughter-nymphs of Nereus. Poseidon's power over the waves is well-known to us through the *Odyssey* when he creates storms to impede Odysseus. Familiar also are the stories of Poseidon's equine progeny: the marvellous winged steed Arion, who was able to speak; and the snowy white, immortal Pegasus, gifted with extraordinary speed, reminiscent of Celtic extraordinary horses from Macha to Morgain.

The time-honoured simile of white-crested breakers looking like the manes of white horses is obviously, in the light of this myth, no superficial analogy. Thus, in the "Ballad of the Equinox" (*The Death Bell,* pp. 72-74), when Watkins describes the destructive sea which "Carries the bones of the dead," even a naturalistic description of the white horses of the sea carries mythic reverberations:

> Beyond Hunt's moonlike bay,
> That pockmarked crescent of rocks,
> White horses, dead white horses,
> Priests of the equinox,
>
> Deride my lonely curse. . . .

Who can doubt that "moonlike" and "crescent" and "priests" endow the white horses—dead ones yet—with mythic, rather than mere metaphoric connotations?

In the "Ballad of the Mari Lwyd," of course, the white horse of the sea is no less than the Mari herself, even in the view of the repudiating Living, whose term "priestlike" is naturally pejorative:

> A white horse frozen blind,
> Hurled from a seawave's hollow,
> Fostered by spray and wind,
> Profane and priestlike thing! (p. 78)

This stanza is reminiscent of an ancient fragment of an elegy of a Leinster prince drowned in his little boat, preserved in the *Annals of Tigernach* s.a. 622, as quoted in Dillon and Chadwick, (p. 144), where metaphor and myth meet in the cursed Morrigan:

> The deep clear depths of the sea and the sand on the sea-bed have covered them. They have hurled themselves over Conaing in his frail little curach. The woman has flung her white mane against Conaing in his curach. Hateful is the laugh which she laughs today.

The sea figures in a large number of Watkins's poems, often—especially in his ballads—a terrible and sinister force. His feeling about its provocative nature, its ambiguity, is expressed in "New Year, 1965" (p. 22), where he comments on the Bristol Channel viewed from his Gower home:

> Sometimes I have seen it, after a stormy night, vast, yet immediate, containing all its contradictions, all its opposing forces in a single harmonious vision. I have never doubted the terror, even the malice of the seas' designs; to see it in a moment of repose is mysterious and supremely satisfying. Water, the source of life, the life-giver, in eternal movement, the perfect mirror, the silent interpreter of death and change, compels both eye and mind with its endless fascination.

In this view of the sea as the maker and breaker of life, the source and end of vitality, Watkins has summed up in naturalistic terms the ambivalence of the sea in the myth of the Great Goddess. She is associated with water not only in her role of Proprietress of the Dead, but as the Creatrix, the Great Mother—aptly enough, since the Earth will surely not produce life unless moisture is present. The sea, indeed, figures in several creation myths as the prime substance of the universe and the origin of life. As Kathleen Raine observes: "The Sea, ancient and universal symbol of material flux, impressed by the 'breath of life' in the beginning, is an image from Genesis, acceptable alike to Platonist and evolutionist" (p. 184). Aquatic symbolism also plays an important part in alchemical lore—the *materia prima* of the primordial chaotic state being fluid.[4] It is not difficult to see how this *materia prima* became equated with the amniotic fluid, and thence why, according to Eliade, "the sacred rivers of Mesopotamia were supposed to have their source in the generative organ of the Great Goddess" (pp. 41, 154-155).

The name "Mari" actually invites etymological connection with the Indo-European base *mori-* or *mari-*, as seen in Greek *meer*, Latin *mare*, Gothic *marei* and in Anglo-Saxon and modern English *mere*. The derivation may not be proved, but mythographers have generally associated names containing "mar" or "mir" with the sea. So one of Freyja's names, Mardoll, is claimed by Davidson to come from *marr*, the sea (p. 116). And Graves speaks of the antecedent of Aphrodite, the Greeks' Love-Goddess born of the sea-foam, and styled Anadyomene, "she who came out of the sea," as the pagan Sea-goddess Mar an, a "charming Virgin with the blue robe and pearl necklace,' who turns up variously as Miriam ("Sea-brine"), Mariamne ("Sea-lamb"), Myrrhine, Myrtea (a title of Aphrodite), and as the May-bride and Maid Marian, as well as the "merry-maid, as 'mermaid' was once written" (pp. 395-397, 262). Graves states that the Gnostics believed that "Mary" meant "of the sea," and conceived of the Virgin as the physical vessel of the Holy Spirit, who m"moved on the face of the waters," in which Christ was conceived and thus made incarnate (p. 157).

In *The Lost Language of Symbolism,* in the discussion of early watermark emblems portraying "Mary, Maria, Myrrha, Miriam, or Mara," as Water-Mothers or mermaids, Harold Bayley notes:

4 See Mircea Eliade, *The Forge and the Crucible,* trans. Stephen Corrin (London, 1962), p. 40.

99

There is hardly a nation whose history has come down to us that does not record the existence of some Saviour God born of an Immaculate Virgin, and not infrequently this Virgin Mother is named Maria or an equivalent word pointing to the Sea. Dionysos was born of the virgin Myrrha; Hermes, the Logos of the Greeks, was born of the virgin Myrrha or Maia, and the mother of the Siamese Saviour was called Maya Maria. All these names are related to Mare, the Sea, and the immaculate purity of the various Mother-Marys is explained by the mystic tenet that Spirit in its element was like water, essentially pure. . . . (I, 235-236)

Elsewhere Bayley notes:

The name Mary is by some writers identified with Miriam, meaning the sad and unfortunate one, the star of the sea, a drop of the sea; others derive it from Mara the Nereid, whose name may express the phosphoric flashing of the surface of the sea just as the anme Maira expresses the sparklings of the dog-star Sirius. (I, 191)

While we are on the subject of the name "Mari," it should be noted that the name in that spelling crops up not only in the Mari or Marie Morgan of Breton folklore, but as one of the ancient names of the Great Goddess in the Fertile Crescent. According to Graves, "Mari was the name of the goddess on whose account the Egyptians of 1000 B.C. called Cyprus "Aymari," and who ruled at Mari on the Euphrates (a city sacked by Hammurabi in 1800 B.C.) and at Amari in Minoan Crete" (p. 371). From 1933 onwards, excavations at Mari uncovered a vast palace containing astonishing murals and other works of art. Zehren describes how one mural shows the Great Goddess wearing a horned crown and standing upright on a lion, "surrounded by representations of trees, animals, hybrids and gods," and "holding, at the level of her breast, a large vessel with a spout," through which water may once have gushed (pp. 80-82).

Graves offers another possible etymology for "Mari." He speculates that it may mean "the fruitful mother" from *Ma*, a shortening of the Sumerian *Ama*, "mother," and *rim*, "to bear a child," adding: "So Mari-ri-enna is 'the fruitful mother of Heaven', alias Miriam, Marian of Mariandyne, the 'leaping Myrrhine' of Troy, and Mariamne: a word of triple power" (p. 371).

The Relationship of the Mari to the Virgin Mary

Returning to a discussion of the attributes of the Mari conveyed in the Ballad, we must focus now on the claims made by the Dead about the Mari which seem to equate her with the Mother of Christ. When they call her "Mari of your sorrows," and claim:

> . . . Mari here is holy;
> She saw dark thorns harrow
> Your God crowned with holly,   (p. 78)

are these of the order of the "holy deceptions" which Watkins, in his note accompanying the Ballad, imputes to the Dead?

Let us take the title "Mari of your sorrows" first. There is nothing deceptive *per se* in this. "Mother of Sorrows" does not have an exclusively Christian connotation. The role of *Mater Dolorosa* belonged to the Great Goddess millennia before Christ was born. As E. O. James asserts, in the seasonal myth she becomes the suffering goddess the moment she does her lover-son to death, as in the Phrygian rites of lamentation of Cybele, whose frenzied priests scourged and mutilated themselves to unite their blood with the Goddess sorrowing for the God Attis, her lover-son-victim (pp. 135, 173). So great was Aphrodite's grief, she would not relinquish the body of Adonis until the gods decreed he could spend half the year in this world, and she half the year with him in the Otherworld. A ceremony of burial observed during the festival celebrated in his honour was accompanied by weeping and wailing, ending with joyful shouts of "Adonis lives, and is risen again!"[5] The death of Osiris was likewise lamented by votaries of the Goddess Isis, meaning, Graves claims "she-who-weeps" (p. 337). How widespread was the theme of the Sorrowing Mother is indicated by the fact that the Norse Frigg and Freyja are also pictured as weeping goddesses.

Similarly, if the Mari *is* an emanation of the Great Goddess, there is nothing deceptive in the Dead's reference to her holiness. Nor need it be understood that as witness of the cruci-

---

5 Alexander Stuart Murray, *Manual of Mythology* (New York, 1891), p. 86. See also Frazer, *Adonis, Attis, Osiris,* throughout.

fixion of Christ she was the *Christian* Virgin or one of the other biblical Marys. The Great Mother's omniscience and ubiquity could have placed her there.

An analysis of the exact words in which the Dead make their claim about the Mari's presence at the Crucifixion reveals that no specifically Christian terms are used. A harrowing among dark thorns is an experience common to all undergoing the mystic "descent," and a crowning with holly, shiny and green in midwinter, thus symbolic of rebirth (like the evergreen myrtle of the Adonis myth), took place in pagan coronations of the Holly King, presumably related to the Divine Star Son reborn at the Winter Solstice. A displacement of this symbol to mark the death of Christ (though followed immediately by his resurrection) led to greater emphasis being place on the holly's thorns than on its evergreenness.

Thus the Dead speak only of the Christian Crucifixion in terms common to pagan beliefs. The Dead can be called deceptive only to the extent that they play on the self-importance and ignorance of the Living in their belief that these details are unique to Christian faith. As readers, too, we must not forget that Calvary (from the Vulgate's *Calvaria*, the Latin for "skull") was Golgotha, a place of skulls (from the Aramaic *Golgolta,* a skull) long before it was the scene of Christ's Crucifixion. From the beginning of time it has been a "skull-shaped hill," the hill, as we have seen, being the symbol and the reality of the Earth Mother, a pregnant belly and a mound of death, the womb-tomb into which the dead returned.[6]

If the Dead *are* cunningly confusing the Christian Mary with the Great Goddess, they are doing no more than many early Christians did, right up to the returning Crusaders tinged with the cult of the Goddess preserved by heretical sects in the Holy Land. The coalescing of the cult of the Earth Mother and the worship of Mary, Mother of God, runs all the way from mild forms of absorption of pagan rites and myths, through Marianism and Mariolatry, to the most unpardonable (from the Church's point of view) heresies such as, in Graves' words, "the

6 For the alchemical concept of *regressus ad uterum,* see Eliade, *The Forge and the Crucible,* pp. 154 ff.

identification of the Hercules-Dionysus-Mithras bull, whose
living flesh the Orphic ascetics tore and ate in their initiation
ceremony, with Jesus Christ whose living flesh was symbolically torn and eaten in Holy Communion," and the
corollary "identification of the Virgin Mary with the Triple
Goddess" (p. 142).

We do not have to believe that the cult of the Christian Mary
is no more than another version of the cult of the Goddess to
recognise how attributes of the Magna Mater could become
attached to the Mother of the Redeemer, especially when
Christian churches were superimposed on sites formerly dedicated to manifestations of the Great Goddess as E. O, Jones
describes (p. 202). Even before the Christian era, some sublima-
tion of the Great Goddess had occurred. The hellenized Isis had
become more and more syncretistic, and in her various
manifestations—as Cybele, Demeter, Athene, Venus—was
purified of the orgiastic elements of the cult. James points out:

> Like the sublime Virgin Mother, who eventually was to dethrone
> her, she was the "goddess of many names," the queen of heaven,
> mother of the stars, first-born of all ages, parent of nature,
> patroness of sailors, star of the sea, and Mater dolorosa, giving
> comfort and consolation to mourners and those in distress, and
> finally . . . "the saviour of the human race," the redemptrix. (pp.
> 179-180)

And after Christ's birth syncretism did not end. Even now,
James declares, devotion to the Madonna of Catholic faith "is
very much more than devotion to the simple, wholly dedicated
peasant maiden of Nazareth." This simple virgin is:

> Nothing less than the Mother of God, the Queen of Heaven, the
> Woman clothed with the sun, having the moon under her feet and
> a crown of twelve stars above her head; and on earth the
> immaculate ever-virgin, the Lily of Eden, the Second Eve, the Star
> of the Sea, the co-redemptress, the compassionate Mother, the
> bestower of grace, the giver of good counsel, Our Lady of Victory.
> (p. 224)

Harold Bayley discusses the process of absorption of one of
these titles:

> Among the titles of Queen Mary is Stella Maris, the Star of the
> Sea—an appellation for which it is difficult to discern any Biblical
> justification. "Star of the Sea" was, however, one of the titles of

Isis, and one must assume that it was sanctioned by Christianity for the usual reason that the people obstinately refused to relinquish it. (I, 235-236).

As Graves notes, the feast of the Assumption of the Blessed Virgin coincides with the feast of Diana, or Vesta (p. 255), and it is no coincidence that the birth of Christ is placed about the time of the winter solstice when the Mithraic festival of light's victory over darkness was celebrated, and when the Egyptian sun-god was born anew in the arms of Isis. It may also be significant that on December 25 at midnight, as James points out, the constellation of Virgo (Latin "virgin"), "symbolizing the Mother-Goddess in Babylonia, gave birth to the life-giving sun" (p. 220). We have already noted that, through association of the stable and the manger with the Christ-child's birth, there may even reside in the Virgin a faint echo of the Goddess as "Divine Horse."

The Night Mare and Her Ninefold

Whether or not the Dead in Watkins's Ballad are deliberately trying to promote their Mari by confusing her with the Virgin Mary, the Living are not taken in. They are well aware of the Mari's identity, and differ only with the Dead about the values to be placed on her. The implications of the title "Queen of the starry fillies," which the Dead confer on their Mare-Goddess, is turned opprobriously against them when the Living denounce the Retinue as "Night-nags foaled of the starry skies/Threatening our feast."

This repudiation is made in the same terms and with the same attitude as those of the Christian Church during the Middle Ages when all vestiges of the pagan horse rites were associated with black magic, the black mass, and witchcraft, and denounced as "demoniacum." This is the sense of the accusation of blasphemous practices made by the Living against the Dead in the poem:

> A starlit crucifix hits their knees
> And a chain of bloodstained beads
> Drops to the fork where the fingers seize
> Their good and evil deeds.
> Those blasphemous hands can change our mind

Or mood with a craftsman's skill;
Under their blessings they blast and blind,
Maim, ravish, and kill.   (p. 83)

To understand this attitude we need to have some knowledge of the decline of the cult of the Great Mother. According to Graves, by the birth of Christ her power had already been dissipated by the ascendant Apollo, her own son. Her triple nature breaks into three discrete entities, sometimes beautiful and benign, as in the Three Graces, the Charities; more often ugly, sinister, and awesome, as in such powerful trios as the Moirae, the Fates, the Norns, the Furies and the Graeae, the Grey ones—the three sisters of the Gorgon (p. 229). Finally her tripled nature tripled again, and she became "enlarged in number though reduced in power, to a bevy of nine little departmental goddesses of inspiration, under the tutelage of the former male twin . . . who finally proclaims himself the Eternal Sun, and the Nine Muses become his ladies-in-waiting" (pp. 392-393). Graves makes his connection of the Muses to the Mare-Goddess through the spring on Helicon, seat of the Muses, named Hippocrene, "The Horse Well," which was horse-shoe-shaped. The legend was that it had been struck by the hoof of the horse Pegasus, whose name means "of the springs of water." Poets were said to drink of Hippocrene for inspiration. . . . But it may be supposed that Hippocrene and Aganippe were originally struck by the moon-shaped hoof of Leucippe ('White Mare'), the Mare-headed Mother herself" (pp. 383-384).

This splintering of the powers of the three-phased Moon into an ennead accounts, in Graves' view, for the colleges of orgiastic priestesses at remote oracular shrines, often on islands, which turn up in various contexts. Graves contends the "most ancient surviving record" of such a sinister ninesome is the Aurignacian cave-painting at Cogus in Spain, which he reads as a crescent of nine wild women, representing various phases of the moon and womanhood from maiden to hag, dancing around the young Dionysus. Closer to us in time Graves cites the Lenaea at Athens—he calls it the "Festival of the Wild Women"—who dramatized the tearing apart of

Dionysus at the winter solstice (p. 399). Graves points also to the "nine orgiastic priestesses of the Island of Sein in West Brittany, and the nine damsels in the *Preiddeu Annwn* whose breaths warmed Cerridwen's cauldron" (p. 391). Indeed, he even calls the Muses themselves "nine orgiastic priestesses of the Moon-goddess" (p. 173), and similarly describes the Sirens (p. 418), which explains men's fascinated fear of them.

Votaries of the Goddess continued to defy the proscriptions of the Church throughout the Middle Ages, meeting in covens on remote heaths to celebrate their fertility rites. In the folklore, as often happens in shamanistic practices, the priestess was identified with the deity, and witches were believed to be demons themselves. These beliefs were reinforced by accounts such as this one, summarized by Davidson:

> One of the early kings of Sweden was said to have been crushed to death by a seidkana who took on the form of a horse. According to *Landnamabok,* a woman skilled in witchcraft was brought to trial in Iceland for "riding" a man to death in a similar way. . . . An English chronicle of the twelfth century states that the wife of King Edgar was accused of witchcraft and that she was accustomed to take on the form of a horse by her magic arts, and was seen by a bishop "running and leaping hither and thither with horses and showing herself shamelessly to them." (pp. 121-122)

Remnants of the horse cult came to light in the witch hunts and trials of more recent centuries. Graves notes that in 1673 Anne Armstrong, a Northumbrian witch, confessed at her trial to having been temporarily transformed into a mare by her mistress Ann Forster of Stockfield, who threw a bridle over her head and rode her to a meeting of five witch-covens at Riding Mill Bridge End (p. 385, n. 1).

Shakespeare's grim threesome in *Macbeth* is just such a coven of witches with shamanistic powers to ride the wind:

> The weird sisters, hand in hand,
> Posters of the sea and land,
> Thus do go about, about:
> Thrice to thine and thrice to mine
> And thrice again, to make up nine . . .   (I, ii, 32)

In the play they operate under the tutelage of Hekate, the Great Goddess of Greek manifestation, in her role of Goddess of the Dead, with her train of ghosts and demons, and her predilection for graveyards and crossroads.

All the sinister significance which the Church built up against remnants of Magna Mater in the Middle Ages, even to attributing to her an exclusively chthonic identity, is applied by the Living to the Mari and to her Retinue in Watkins's Ballad.

Another reference in Shakespeare to the residual rites of the horse cult preserved in folklore casts light on the Ballad. In his babblings, King Lear claims that when St. Swithhold "footed thrice the wold":

> He met the Night-Mare and her nine-fold,
> Bid her alight and her troth plight,
> And Aroynt thee, witch, aroynt thee!   (III, iv, 126 ff.)

Here the Night-Mare is clearly the Mare-Goddess. Her nine-fold nature is seized here either as a retinue of spirits, or, since she is herself designated a witch, an ennead of orgiastic priestesses, or a coven of witches. Clearly by Shakespeare's day, though Christianity had succeeded in depreciating her to the level of an evil force, it had failed to stamp her out completely.

The jibe of the Living in the Ballad that the Dead are "night nags" undoubtedly implies an allusion to the nine-fold train of the sinister Mare-Goddess. It is also in this primary sense of the word "night-mare" that we must understand the observation of the Voice in the Ballad:

> Out in the night the nightmares ride;
> And the nightmares' hooves draw near . . .   (p. 76)

Obsolete except in the modern word "nightmare" (whose original connotation is all but forgotten) the word "mare" is still listed in Webster's Dictionary with the definition "a hag or goblin supposed to suffocate people during sleep, an incubus." The most primitive of totemic concepts is implicit in this sense of the "Mare"—the belief that the creative spirit of the totem propagates the tribe by entering and impregnating its women.

107

In the treatise *Of Ghostes and Spirites Walking by Night,* 1572,
Lewes Lavater calls them *"Ephialtae and Hyphialtae,* that is
Incubi and Succubi (which we call Maares) . . . night spirits or
rather Diuells, which leaps upon men in their sleepe," though
by this date he, and others, were beginning to diagnose them as
a disease of the mind.

Howey gives us this interesting summary of the activities of
the Night Mare:

> It is interesting to find that what we call a nightmare was believed
> by our ancestors to be the result of a visitation from the Saxon
> demon Mare or Mara. This was a sort of vampire which sat on the
> chest of its sleeping victim, half strangling him and causing fear-
> ful visions. The phrase "Away the mare" has reference to this
> incubus. . . . These demon nightmares were supposed to guard
> hidden treasures when not occupied . . . and over these they would
> brood as a hen over her eggs. Hence comes the saying, "A Mare's
> nest," meaning the spot where the vampire mounts guard over
> concealed stores of good things.   (p. 44)

Graves gives us this composite picture of the Night Mare
culled from many sources and cemented with his imagination in
his own inimitable way:

> The Night Mare is one of the cruellest aspects of the White
> Goddess. Her nests, when one comes across them in dreams,
> lodged in rock-clefts or the branches of enormous hollow yews,
> are built of carefully chosen twigs, lined with white horse-hair and
> the plumage of prophetic birds and littered with the jaw-bones
> and entrails of poets. . . . (p. 26)

He gives this further description:

> If the visitant is the Nightmare, the poet will recognize her by the
> following signs. She will appear as a small mettlesome mare, not
> more than thirteen hands high, of the breed familiar from the
> Elgin marbles: cream-coloured, clean-limbed, with a long head,
> bluish eye, flowing mane and tail. Her nine-fold will be nine fillies
> closely resembling her. .
> Her speed when she sets her ears back is indeed wonderful; no tall
> thoroughbred on earth can long keep her pace—proof of which is
> the pitiable condition in which hag-ridden horses used to be found
> at cock-crow in the stables from which they had been stolen for a
> midnight frolic—in a muck-sweat, panting like bellows, with

7 Ed. J. Dover Wilson and May Yardley (Oxford, 1929), pp. 6 and 12-13.

bleeding sides and foam on their lips, nearly foundered.
Let the poet address her as Rhiannon, "Great Queen," and avoid
the discourtesy of Odin and St. Swithold. . . . She will respond
with a sweet complaisance and take him the round of her nests. (p.
420)

One more quotation will provide interesting background for
Watkins's poem. In Harrison Ainsworth's novel *Rookwood* is a
poem titled "Ephialtes" meaning "one who leaps" and, as we
have seen, a synonym for the Night Mare. There, the Mare's
hag aspect, the moonless night (the dead phase of the moon),
the white horse, the imagery of ice and freezing cold, and the
assault of the incubus, provide valuable associations:

> I am the hag who rides by night
> Through the moonless air on a courser white!
> Over the dreaming earth I fly
> Here and there—at my phantasy!
> My frame is withered, my visage old,
> My looks are frore, and my bones ice-cold,
> The wolf will howl as I pass his lair,
> The ban-dog moan, and the screech-owl stare.
> For breath at my coming the sleeper strains,
> And the freezing current forsake his veins.
> Vainly for pity the wretch may sue—
> Merciless Mara no prayers subdue.
>
> To his couch I flit—
> On his breast I sit;
>   Astride! astride! astride!
> And one charm alone
> (A hollow stone)
>   Can scare me from his side.[8]

Sexual assault by incubi was a Celtic as well as a Saxon
belief, the Celts calling them *dusii,* according to MacCulloch
(p. 14). Viewed as an attenuation of the Great Mother, the
Night Mare, of course, would have been a succubus, which connects her again to the orgiastic ninesomes from whom a man —
even Odysseus — must flee if he values his life.

There is no implication in Watkins's Ballad that the Mari is
so disposed. The Dead, however, assert—without in any way

---

8 Quoted by Howey, pp. 47-48. The "hollow stone" is the "holy," "halig," or
  "hag" stone worn as a talisman around the neck, or hung in stables to
  protect horses from being stolen for midnight capers.

implicating the Mari—that just as she knows everything else, she knows the ways of the *incubi*;

'Under the womb of teeming night
Our Mari tries your faith;
And She has Charity's crown of light;
Spectre she knows and wraith;
How sweet-tongued children are wickedly born
By a swivelling devil's thrust
Mounting the night with a murderous horn,
Riding the starry gust.'   (p. 80)

We are struck by the tantalizing closeness of the name Mari to the proper name "Mare" or "Mara" given to the Night Mare, and again we are reminded of Marie Trevelyan's speculation that Mari may really be *Marw,* the Welsh for "death." Nor do the associations end there, for the name "Mara" also occurs in Hindu and Buddhist speculation as the personal embodiment of the powers of evil:

He is hostile to men, tempting, deceiving, and terrifying them, that he may lead deluded mortals to death and keep them in the toils of ignorance and desire. He is the great demon of earthly desire and death.[9]

It is interesting that the name Mari can provoke so many proper names with connotations both adverse and positive (as outlined in previous sections), enhancing the effect of the "reconciliation of contraries, an eternal moment of contradictions" that Watkins wanted to achieve.

The terror fanned in Christian souls by the Goddess of Death and the demon witches or night mares who conjured her up, who indulged in aberrant and sacrilegious practices with her, and who rode the winds with her, is captured in the following nightmare threat which the Dead make to the Living:

'O who has woven the skein of the hair,
And who has knotted the ropes of the fist,
And who has hollowed the bones of the eyes?
One of you answer: the hands have kissed.
I see in your eyes white terror,
I see in your locked hands hate.'   (p. 81)

9 Shailer Mathews and Gerald Birney Smith, *A Dictionary of Religion and Ethics* (New York, 1923), p. 271.

But here the power of the Mari is actually couched in terms of the Great Goddess's manifestation as the threefold Fates or Norns, who have the terrible, inexorable power to spin or weave each man's destiny at birth.

Wind, Breath, and the Goddess of Inspiration

The "night nags" and the "swivelling devil" alluded to in Watkins's ballad are said to do what all sinister powers and their ministers do in folklore rooted in paganism and overlaid with Christian values: they ride the "starry gust." Witches on their flying broomsticks, shamans on their steeds of winged horse or bird, all negotiate space by riding the wind. Where does this folk belief come from? Partly, undoubtedly, from the negative naturalistic associations of gale and wintry blast; partly from the association of the pagan Great Goddess with the winds in her wintry manifestation of Cardea of the Polar Hinge, keeper of the four winds, especially Boreas, and from the associations of such pagan gods as the Brenin Llwyd and Odin with his Valkyries flying across time and space.

How do these sinister forces of folklore marshal this wind-power? Graves says: "Whistling three times in honour of the White Goddess is the traditional witch way of raising the wind" (p. 435), and quotes *Macbeth's* witches—"I'll give thee a wind./And I another"—as well as citing Coleridge's "beautifully exact" account of the Nightmare Life-in-Death who "whistles thrice" after her game of dice for a magical breeze to save the Mariner's life.

Something of these beliefs, embodied in Welsh country superstitions which proscribe whistling in certain circumstances, may lie behind the following exchange between the Living and the Dead. To the claim of the Dead that the Mari can "tame beasts unrully," the Living sneeringly retort:

> She should have been a whistle
> For that tames our collie;
> He darts on like an arrow,
> Then he creeps up slowly. (p. 79)

The jibe, of course, contains a reference to the use of the whistle in training the Welsh sheep dog, the collie, to herd sheep on the Welsh mountains, as seen at sheep dog trials in country fairs and gatherings. But the Dead parry this sneer with:

> 'O, if she were a whistle
> She would not call your collie,
> But through this keyhole narrow
> Try, your wits to rally.' (p. 79)

What the Dead are doing here is exploiting the taunt to establish the positive values of breath and wind in association with the Goddess. The close connection between "breath" and "spirit" and "inspiration" occurs in many languages. Latin *spiritus*, for example, from *spirare*, to breathe, means breath, breath of a god, and inspiration. When the body dies, the breath goes out of it to become a spirit; when shaman or poet is inspired he is breathing in the breath of a god, or spirit. Graves contends that the poetic condition, which he considers to be a paranoiac trance in which time is suspended, can be induced by "listening to the wind, the messenger of the Goddess Cardea, in a sacred grove" (pp. 440, 435 ff., and 158 ff.). The importance of the Aeolian harp in Romantic theories of poetic inspiration derives from this belief.[10]

From our discussion in previous chapters it may seem that the hag aspect of the Great Goddess (that aspect of her in her phase of the dead moon, of the dead season of the year, and the dead of night, in short, in her role as Goddess of Destruction and Death) dominates Watkins's Ballad. But by cleverly turning this wisecrack, intended by the Living to ridicule the Mari, into an attribute characterizing the Mari's inspirational powers, the Dead remind us of the creative aspect of the Goddess (the waxing moon, the girl and woman of spring and summer). These creative powers are not simply creative in the sense that she gives birth—and rebirth—to all of nature. She has the power to generate understanding and to increase know-

---

10 For the importance of whistling in shamanistic practice, see Hays, p. 156; Rees and Rees, p. 362. Evans-Wentz, p. 208, says Breton corrigans whistle to assemble.

ledge. She can inspire insight, prophetic and poetic visions, and new art forms. In short, she presides over all acts of generation of any kind.

It is to that side of her creativity that the Dead refer when they imply their Mari, as the spirit of a god, can insinuate her way in the guise of a whistle through the keyhole and "rally the wits" of the Living within. It is of that divine power they speak when they promise the Living the gift of inspiration and light from the Mari:

> 'And now you must let our Mari in:
> She must inspire your feast.' (p. 74)

and:

> 'Great light you shall gather . . ." (p. 78)

Countering the implications of the Living that the Mari is a sinister vestige of an abhorrent pagan religion, the Dead claim that the Mari, far from practising the black art of witches, exercises an art which is white—pure and sublime:

> 'Hers the white art that rouses
> Light in the darkest places.' (p. 78)

Thus, they argue, although they themselves may appear "black as a mole's burrow," truly they "come to bless," for their own inspiration has come from this Mari with dominion over the triple realms of sky, seas and land:

> 'Our wit is come from the seawave's roar,
> The stars and the stinging hail.' (p. 74)

The Relationship of the Welsh Cerridwen to Watkins's Mari

The Greek Goddess of Inspiration in her weakened nine-fold manifestation of the Muses is well known to us. But of far greater importance to a full reading of Watkins's Ballad is the Welsh Manifestation of the Great Goddess called Cerridwen (or Cyridwen, or Caridwen), sometimes regarded as one of three daughters who came out of the cauldron of Ogyrven, or Ogyr Vran—otherwise Bran—credited by the Welsh bards with inventing the elements of their art: language, poetry, and the letters of the alphabet.[11] However sired, Cerridwen is considered to be far more ancient than other Welsh manifestations of the Great Goddess: Rhiannon, Arianrhod, Blodeuwedd and Olwen. Cerridwen was a Sow-Demeter, predecessor of the Mare-Demeter, according to Graves, devourer of her own children, and an elemental corn goddess. As *Hen Wen,* the "Old White One," she was the sinister old hag, the Goddess in her destructive phase. But it is as primordial creatrix, possessor of the Celtic Cauldron of Inspiration, that she is most renowned. The Cauldron is the same one that Bran gave to Matholwych in the Second Branch of the *Mabinogi* to restore life to the dead. According to such authorities as MacCulloch it is the forerunner of the Holy Grail of Arthurian Legend. It is also related to the sacred vessel or the sacred Vase in the rites of Cybele and Isis, the container or chalice of the intoxicating Soma or wine, or life-giving water; or conceived of as matrix or womb, and, in the case of intellectual generation, as the brain.[12] In the attenuated form of the cult of the Goddess in mediaeval witchcraft, it is the cauldron in which witches brew their evil potions, as in Act IV of *Macbeth.*

About the Celtic name of "the White Sow, the Barley-Goddess, the White Lady of Death and Inspiration" Graves writes:

> Her name is composed of the words *cerdd* and *wen. Wen* means "white," and *cerdd* in Irish and Welsh means "gain" and also "the inspired arts, especially poetry," like the Greek words *cerdos* and *cerdeia,* from which derives the Latin *cerdo,* a craftsman. (pp. 67-68)

11 See MacCulloch, both in *Mythology of All Races,* Celtic III, p. 112, and in *The Religion of the Ancient Celts,* p. 383. Graves cites an interseting fusion of pagan and Christian belief when thirteen- and fourteenth- century bards used a play on words to refer to the Virgin Mary as the source of inspiration. The secondary form of the Welsh *pair,* cauldron, on assuming the soft form of its initial is *mair,* which also means Mary in Welsh (p. 394). Also see Graves pp. 76 and 383 to 385.
12 Mary Esther Harding, *Woman's Mysteries* (New York, 1955), pp. 136 ff. See also: Eliade, *The Forge and the Crucible,* pp. 154, 118, 40, etc.; Frazer, *Adonis, Attis, Osiris,* II, 274.

Perhaps similar etymological deductions, especially of the syllable "wen," worked in Watkins's imagination to weave the lines: "Hers the white art that rouses/Light in the darkest palace" (p. 73).

Since most of what we know about Cerridwen is detailed in "The Romance of Taliesin," which Lady Charlotte Guest translated and included in her version of *The Mabinogion* (pp. 263 ff.), let us turn to this story. It begins with an account of Cerridwen (Lady Charlotte Guest spells it "Caridwen") boiling up a cauldron of Inspiration and Science to equip her son Afagddu with "knowledge of the mysteries of the future state of the world," as a compensation for his ugliness.

Even in the myth-degraded mediaeval manuscript, Cerridwen possesses all the occult knowledge of "the books of the astronomers" and of Fferyllt (Virgil). She knows the planetary hours, the magical and medicinal value of all plants and herbs, and the proper incantations and spells to produce her inspired brew, through which she exerts her godlike powers over man and beast. Recognizing these unique gifts, Lady Charlotte observes in a note to the text, that with her Cauldron of Inspiration, or the Awen, "Caridwen is generally considered to be the Goddess of Nature of Welsh mythology" (p. 429).

Watkins's Mari, if we are to believe the claims of the Dead, has similar gifts:

'She has those precious secrets
Known to the minstrel solely,
Experienced in the marrow,
Quick to tame beasts unruly.' (pp. 78-79)

That which is "experienced in the marrow"—the vital substance—is that kind of knowing treated in the discussion of the "dreaming mare" above, wherein will and intellect play no part.[13] In beings possessing will and intellect what is experienced in the marrow goes by the name of intuition, a more

13 Cf. Yeats: "God guard me from those thoughts men think / In the mind alone. / He that sings a lasting song / Thinks in a marrow bone." From "A Prayer for Old Age" (first published in the *Spectator* in 1934) *The Collected Poems of W. B. Yeats* (New York, 1965), p. 281.

creative power than the rational faculties, a power that attunes the shaman to his deity, poet to his muse.

"The "Romance of Taliesin" goes on to tell that, by accident "as Caridwen was culling plants and making incantations," three precious drops of inspiration fell on Gwion, a little boy whom she had set to stir the cauldron. Putting the finger scalded by the "marvel-working drops" into his mouth, he foresaw everything that was to come. The precious potion, however, was turned into poison and lost.

Thereupon, a transformation combat ensued, Gwion putting himself through a number of magical shape-shifts to escape the ire of Cerridwen, who herself changed shape to suit:

> And she went forth after him, running. And he saw her and changed himself into a hare and fled. She changed herself into a greyhound and turned him. And he ran towards the river, and became a fish. And she in the form of an otter-bitch chased him under the water, until he was fain to turn himself into a bird of the air. She, as a hawk, followed him and gave him no rest in the sky. (p. 264).

Finally, Gwion turns himself into an ear of grain on her threshing floor. Cerridwen transforms herself to a hen and promptly swallows him. Nine months later she delivers him, but finding him too beautiful to kill, she casts him in the ocean in a leathern bag. He washes up into the Weir of Gwyddno between Dyfi and Aberystwyth, and is saved by Gwyddno's son Elphin, who names Gwion "Taliesin," Radiant Brow. Taliesin proves an inspired bard.

Thereafter, the story is Taliesin's but since his powers derive from Cerridwen's power, whatever defines him defines her. Moreover, as will become apparent, many of Taliesin's songs which are incorporated in the narrative of the "Romance" must have been echoing in Watkins's mind as he conceived his Mari.

First, upon his liberation from the bag, Taliesin sings Elphin a "Consolation" in which Taliesin describes himself as having special gifts and powers:

> Although I am but little, I am highly gifted. (p. 265)

And:

> There lies a virtue in my tongue.
> While I continue thy protector
> Thou hast not much to fear; (p. 266)

116

When asked "what he was, whether man or spirit," Taliesin recounts his pursuit by Cerridwen, and his transformation into many more shapes than the narrative has detailed, as crow, roe, wolf, squirrel, iron, bull, boar, and so on, ending the catalogue:

> I have fled as a white grain of pure wheat,
> On the skirt of a hempen sheet entangled,
> That seemed of the size of a mare's foal,
> That is filling like a ship on the waters;   (p. 267)

Obliquely, these lines seem to echo the corn-mare deity, and the final lines:

> Into a dark leathern bag I was thrown,
> And on a boundless sea I was sent adrift;
> Which was to me an omen of being tenderly nursed,
> And the Lord God then set me at liberty   (p. 267)

have resonances of the sea as the source of life, and of the miraculous birth of divine infants from some ark upon the waters, resonances continued in the first line of the next song:

> In water there is a quality endowed with a blessing;   (p. 267)

This song goes on to state Taliesin's powers of reincarnation:

> Three times have I been born, I know by meditation;   (p. 267)

and his magical gift of all-knowledge, derived from Cerridwen:

> All the sciences of the world, collected together in
>   my breast.   (p. 267)

In yet another poem, he claims the power of poetry strong enough to silence the court bards and to free Elphin, who has been imprisoned for boasting of those very powers of Taliesin:

> The hall I will enter,
> And my song I will sing;
> My speech I will pronounce
> To silence royal bards.   (p. 271)

and he actually does "set kind Elphin free" with "a sapient Druid's words," robbing the royal bards of power of utterance except to play "blerwm, blerwm" on their lips.

117

Let us pause here to observe that by virtue of such claims some mythologists, such as Graves, have seen Taliesin to be a Divine Son in the myth of the Corn-and-Mare Goddess. The Divine Son, who has as many manifestations and names as the Divine Mother—Dionysus, Hercules, Orpheus, Osiris, Diarmaid—is, as we have seen, the Spirit of the Year born to his Virgin mother at the winter solstice, to become successively her lover and her victim. When he is slain by her, his tanist, weird, or twin—the God of the Waning Year—takes his place until he, as God of the Waxing Year, is resurrected to begin the seasonal cycle all over again (p. 110 ff., 125 ff.).

Whether or not the songs in the "romance" were written by a bard of the name of Taliesin (and such a bard does appear to have lived in the sixth century), the substance of the songs seems, in J. A. MacCulloch's view, to involve "mythical elements which introduce old divinities, a culture hero or god, Taliesin," and should be read as assertions by the persona of the poems that "he has been with the gods and ranks himself as one of them, telling how he was created and enchanted by them before he became immortal." McCulloch continues: "Taliesin was the ideal bard, a god of inspiration like Ogma, and besides his reincarnation, his birth from Cerridwen shows his divine nature" (p. 111). Graves believes that the "I" of the Taliesin poems "is the Apollo-like god on whose behalf the inspired poet sings, not the poet himself" (p. 100), and shares MacCulloch's view that Taliesin's having become a grain of corn swallowed by the hag Cerridwen identifies him as a Barley-god (p. 136).

Let us see how Cerridwen-Taliesin may be a prototype for Watkins's Mari. The narrative of the "Romance" tells that when the three drops of inspiration fell on Gwion-Taliesin, "he foresaw everything that was to come," and in one of his songs he asserts: "For I know what has been, what in future will occur (p. 267)." We have already seen that the Dead claim for the Mari similar omniscience: "For she knows all from the birth of the Flood/To this moment where we stand (p. 74)."

And consider these lines from a song sung by Taliesin to the king, who enquired "what he was, and whence he came," noting both the star references and the persona's ubiquity:

Primary chief bard am I to Elphin,
And my original country is the region of the summer stars;
Idno and Heinin called me Merddin,
At length every king will call me Taliesin.

I was with my Lord in the highest sphere,
On the fall of Lucifer into the depth of hell
I have borne a banner before Alexander;
I know the names of the stars from north to south;
I have been on the galaxy at the throne of the Distributor;
I was in Canaan when Absalom was slain;
I conveyed the Divine Spirit to the level of the vale of Hebron;
I was in the court of Don before the birth of Gwidion.
. . . .
I was at the place of the crucifixion of the merciful Son of God;
I have been three periods in the prison of Arianrod;
. . . .
I have been in the firmament with Mary Magdalene;
I have obtained the muse from the cauldron of Caridwen;   (p. 273)

Now consider the following description from the Ballad
detailing how the Dead have accompanied the Mari across the
universe and across time. Can we doubt that the above lines
were reverberating in Watkins's imagination as he created
them?

'We bring from white Hebron
And Ezekiel's Valley,
From the dead sea of Harlech
And mountain-girt Dolgelley,
All that singing way
From Cader to Kidwelly,
A stiff, a star-struck thing
Blown by the stinging spray
And the stinging light of the stars,
Our white, stiff thing,
Death and breath of the frost,
That has known the room of glass,
Dropped by the Milky Way
To the needle and thread of the pass.'   (p. 77)

What determined Watkins's choice of place names in this
passage? Some choices are obvious now, as the mention of the
vale of Hebron and its association with the Divine Spirit, as
revealed in the Taliesin excerpt above. Not only did Abraham

receive there the vision in which the Lord promised him a son, but as another Taliesin poem sings, Adam was purported to have been created there:

> The Almighty made,
> Down the Hebron vale,
> With his plastic hands,
> Adam's fair form: (pp. 281-2)

Why is Ezekiel's Valley singled out? Perhaps because this Valley of the Dry Bones—so named elsewhere in the poem—is likewise associated with the "white art" of vision and prophecy, as well as with death. There the Lord commanded Ezekiel: "Prophesy upon these bones, and say unto them, O ye dry bones, hear the word of the Lord" (Ezekiel 37.1 ff). It was there that the Lord gave Ezekiel the power to stir the bones to life so that a whole army, the whole house of Israel stood on their feet. It was there the Lord promised: "I will open your graves, and cause you to come up out of your graves, and bring you into your own land." Corroborating this gloss are lines spoken by the Living to the Dead further on in the poem:

> Go back to Cader Idris,
> To your Dry Bones Valley.   (p. 79)

Why is Cader Idris mentioned as a place where the Dead and the Mari have been? The name means "The Chair of Idris," one of the highest summits in Wales, called after a legendary astronomer who studied the stars from its peak. It is also a place of inspiration and ecstatic frenzy, and legend has it that whoever spends a night there will be found next morning a corpse, a madman or a bard.

The "dead sea of Harlech" may also have come to Watkins by way of the Taliesin saga. A note in Lady Charlotte's version mentions that a low-lying territory around Harlech in the realm of Gwyddno, Elphin's father, was overwhelmed by the sea (pp. 429-430). The note also speaks of a poem in the Myvyrian Archaeology (1.165) describing "the outcry of the perishing inhabitants of that unhappy region."

The high and low of Cader and Harlech are matched by two places which appear to come from the modern context—the town of Dolgelly surrounded by mountains, and the seaport of Kidwelly lying on the coast northwest of Gower. It should be noted in passing that Dolgelly/Kidwelly is an eye-rhyme only, since the double "l" in Dolgelly takes the Welsh pronouncia- tion, and Kidwelly the English.

This high-low journey of the Mari across the universe and across the millennia suggests the symbolism of initiation and renaissance mystiques. The Mari, however, unlike her votaries, does not have to struggle and suffer to make contact with the Otherworld. Having "known the room of glass," having been "dropped by the Milky Way" she is at home there, and the "needle and thread of the pass" is the way out of that world, as, for the shaman, it is the way in—the enormously difficult-to- negotiate passage or gateway, like the Symplegades, or like the mere crevice between sky and earth, old and new years, of the *Upanishads.*[14]

14 Mircea Eliade, *Rites and Symbols of Initiation,* p. 65. For the ritual of the "Needle's Eye," see Rees and Rees, p. 98.

CHAPTER VI

THE "BALLAD OF THE MARI LWYD"
IN TOTO

What is Watkins doing with the old myth in the previous chapters? Is the Ballad a mere antiquarian's description of an ancient rite? Or has myth and rite been reworked for metaphysical implications of immediate and urgent relevance to this age? And if the latter, is Watkins recommending some kind of restoration of pagan belief to current practice? Is he promoting the ancient Earth Mother over the paternal God of Judaism and Christianity? Or does he stand with the Living in repudiating the Mari and the Dead as sinister vestiges of an evil superstition? Now that we have a better grasp of the background and allusions we must seek the "statement" of the total poem.

True to form, the Ballad has strong affinities with the drama. As in drama, we must be wary of attributing an authorial position to individual expressions of the *dramatis personae*. As we have seen, the Dead are the Mari's advocates; but before we can accept their testimony, we must certify the reliability of their witness. As we have seen, the Living impugn the Dead and scorn their claims about the Mari. How reliable is *their* testimony? We must also be aware of the possibility of a change of views in the progression of the conflict, and even more wary of awarding central significance to any isolated speech.

The Testimony of the Living

First let us examine and evaluate the testimony of the Living. The first assessment of the character of the Dead is made by the Third Figure in the lighted room where the feast is spread. He begins inauspiciously—with a preconception, a demand, that the Dead *ought* to come back in an attitude of penitence and devoutness. Instead, he charges (in a series of leading questions and without benefit of having yet heard what the Dead have to say) they come back as devils, criminals, gamblers and drunkards:

> Bones of the dead should come on their knees
> Under a pilgrim's cloak,
> But out in the dark what devils are these
> That have smelt our kitchen-smoke?
> Listen. Listen. Who comes near?
> What man with a price on his head?
> What load of dice, what leak in the beer
> Has pulled your steps from the dead?   (p. 73)

To the first appeal of the Dead that they be let in because they have already, at the inn, been denied one meal, and because the Mari can inspire the feast, the Living respond with hearsay prejudice about the hunger, jealousy, drunkenness and ruffianism of the Dead, as well as about their hypocrisy (of "their white hands joined in prayer") and their uncoothness (in ripping "the seams of their proper white clothes"):

> Go back. We have heard of dead men's bones
> That hunger out in the air.
> Jealous they break through their burial-stones,
> Their white hands joined in prayer.
> They rip the seams of their proper white clothes
> And with red throats parched for gin,
> With buckled knuckles and bottle-necked oaths
> They hammer the door of an inn.   (p. 74)

The Dead make an appeal for pity for the distance in time and space they have come, and for the awesomeness of their experience. But the Living pay no heed; they merely repeat their charges. When the Dead withdraw, ending the first "movement" of the poem, the Living reveal a tendency for self-deception—they try to persuade themselves they have not been threatened at all.

> It was the trick of the turning tide
> That brought those voices near.   (p. 76)

123

In the second "movement" of the poem, when the Dead return, the Living are even more scornful, calling them "those fellows," and increasing the charges to include lechery and bastardy:

> Men of the night with a legion of wrongs,
> Fists in the dark that shudder with shame
> Hated lechers with holy songs,
> Bastard bodies that bear no name. (p. 77)

There is a whiff of puritanical Welsh Nonconformity in this identification of the night with lust and shame rather than awe and dread. To the charge of depravity and impiety, the Living add the ultimate charge of evilness: paganism. For the Dead come back "Giving the stars another name," investing them with the luster and power of old gods, "blowing them up with a pair of bellows/From a jumping, thumping, murderous flame."

With this repeated evidence of their blindness and narrowness our sympathy for the Living begins to wane so that by the time the Living and the Dead engage in their exchange of quatrains in the middle "movement" of the poem over the nature and worth of the Mari, we are prepared, as readers, to give the Dead a fair hearing. And if we understand the myth of the Earth Mother, as outlined above, we are prepared to give as much weight to the Dead's case for the sanctity of the Mari as to the Living's repudiation of the White Spirit as mere "froth from a barrel" (p. 78).

Towards the end of this second movement, when the Living repeat their demand that the Dead go back with their "drowned and drunken eyes" to where they came from, their scorn betrays the values of the materialist—you're no good to us because you haven't got anything to give us:

> If we lift and slide the bolt in the door
> What can our warm beer buy?
> What can you give for the food we store
> But a slice of starving sky? (p. 81)

The Dead respond to this insult with an oblique threat about their power to harm, which, if the Dead are to be believed, brings terror to the eyes of the Living. But the "movement" ends

124

immediately with the second retreat of the Dead, and the Living repeat their rationalization that "it was a trick of the turning tide/That brought those voices near" (p. 82).

In the last "movement," the Living confess fear of the "bones of the dead with their crooked eyes/And their crooked mouths so small," and their "picklock tread," while at the same time trying again to deny their existence by casting them in the role of the more manageable threat of thieves in disguise:

> We face the terrible masquerade
> Of robbers dressed like the dead.   (p. 82)

But finally they can only cope with their very real terror by taking a hard and righteous line, diagnosing the persuasive power of the Dead as a malign force which hides itself behind the trappings of holiness, or perverts Christian symbols to blasphemous ends, as do witches celebrating the black mass, a position which has been discussed in the section on the Night Mare. Recognition of the seductive power of that evil ritual, they imply, is the only way they can resist the influence of "those blasphemous hands" which "can change our mind/Or mood with a craftsman's skill." And they convince themselves once and for all of the Dead's sinister hypocrisy:

> Under their blessing they blast and blind,
> Maim, ravish, and kill.   (p. 83)

With this the climax is reached and passed. The Living have argued away the possibility that the Dead or the Mari have anything of value to offer for their lives. Thereafter they repeat their earlier charges and "begones" in the same words, ending with the strongest charge of all, that the Dead are manifestations of a Christian-type Hell:

> Go back to your Hell, there are clean souls here,
> Go back to your barns of muck.
> Go back to your Hell, and leave our beer,   (p. 86)

A cynical sneer is their parting shot:

> And your Mari bring you luck.   (p. 86)

125

The Living then crown their abuses with a threat of physical violence:

> We'll feel you with stones, we'll strip you clean
> In the stars, if you're not gone.   (p. 86)

Yet, when the Dead respond to this threat by leaving, the terror of the Living, which had been momentarily suppressed by self-righteous indignation, breaks through again at the sight of them disappearing into thin air—a phenomenon ironically confirming that the Dead did indeed walk:

> But Jesus! why are you all unseen
> On whom our lamplight shone?   (p. 86)

Altogether, the Living have shown themselves to be prejudiced, self-serving, self-deceiving, self-righteous, and materialistic; the verdict has to be that their testimony about the Dead is not reliable. Finding it too uncomfortable to believe what the Dead had to say, they had to try to deny their existence, to ignore them, and when that didn't work they chose to repudiate their message and power as evil to be resisted.

The Testimony of the Dead

But this does not necessarily mean that the Dead are any more reliable than the Living. That they are hungry and thirsty and jealous of the comforts of the Living is clear from their petitions and actions. In the first "movement" of the poem, they use the classical appeal to pity to try to get what they want. First they complain of having been turned away, starving, from the inn. Then they moan about the awful distance they have come, from places in Welsh history (Harlech and Machynlleth) and Biblical history (En-gedi), suffering great hardships and fear in the cause of Good, and witnessing such great events as David's defeat of Goliath, and Samson's heroic onslaught against the Philistines with an ass's jaw (p. 75).

When that rhetorical bid for pity fails, they try in the second "movement" to argue to the Living the necessity of giving the

Mari entrance on the grounds that she is holy and all-powerful, as we have seen. Then when that fails, they angrily lash out at the Living, thereby seeming to corroborate the very nature the Living have imputed to them, uttering this curse:

> But brightest brimstone light on him
> And burn his rafters black
> That will not give when his fears are dim
> The treasure found in the sack.' (p. 80)

Next they try dire warnings: the Mari is a power that the Living dare not lose; the Mari has the power to see everything, including the sins of the Living—a power which the Dead share—which has been elaborated above. And when that doesn't work they try chiding the Living for their sybaritic escapism and self-deception, saying:

> 'We heard the fire-irons stirring the bars,
> Laying the ash of the grave.
> We saw your faith in the pin of the tongs
> Laying your fears at rest;
> You buried our bones with your drinking-songs
> And murdered what you love best.' (p. 80)

Then their tone becomes graver. It is not the pin of the tongs used to put coal on the fire—thus the symbol of material ease and comfort—that should be exercising the attention of the Living, but the pivot of all existence—that moment when the clock ticks over from the old to the new year, the point when time actually stops—goes out, like a light—the solemn "moment of conscience" when past and present meet, and the ashes of the dead twitch—come to life—roused by the "breaking of bread":

> 'But the pin goes in to the inmost dark
> Where the dead and living meet,
> And the clock is stopped by the shock of the spark
> Or the stealthy patter of sleet
> Where disdain has cast to its utmost pitch
> The strands of the finished thread,
> The clock goes out, and the ashes twitch,
> Roused by the breaking of bread.' (pp. 80-81)

127

The "breaking of bread" must surely suggest more than the supper which the Living are enjoying in celebration of the New Year. It must mean more even than the supper of folk tradition in Celtic culture, when food is left on the hearth or outside the door for the dead to enjoy when they walk on "Spirit Nights." The term "breaking of bread" is the Biblical term for the sacrament of the Eucharist—the ritual ordained by Christ himself for Christian celebrants to partake of His Body and Blood by eating sanctified bread and wine.

Actually, the breaking of bread is not exclusively associated with the Christian Eucharist as Western Christendom mistakenly believes. The Feast of Unleavened Bread, an addition to the Paschal blood ritual of the Hebrews, represents a ritual union of man with his god,[1] just as did the communion meal referred to in the following confession by votaries of Cybele, wherein they ate, in all probability, "a cake of barley meal or of some other grain," which "symbolized the body of the god, son of the mother," and drank either blood or "wine as a symbol of blood":

> I have eaten from the timbrel,
> I have drunk from the cymbal,
> I have borne the sacred vessel,
> I have entered into the bridal chamber.[2]

We know of the star son's association with the fruits of the corn and the vine, from the Dionysian myth, and Frazer has described sacramental meals associated with folk customs of the spirit of the corn.[3]

From an orthodox Christian point of view (especially the narrow-minded conformism of the Living) this suggestion by the Dead that the turning point between old and new years is a moment for sacramental communion between the living and the dead might sound heretical. But readers who have a feeling for the mtaphoric validity of all myth and for the community of

---

1 E. O. James, *The Nature and Function of Priesthood* (New York, 1955), pp. 157 ff. pp. 167 ff.
2 Harding, p. 136, quoting from records of Clement of Alexandria.
3 *Adonis, Attis, and Osiris,* II, 274.

myth—as discussed above—will give credit to the Dead. Then, when the Living ask the materialistic question "What's in it for us if we let you in?" the response of the Dead holds more validity and authority than a petty threat:

'O who has woven the skein of the hair,
And who has knotted the ropes of the fist,
And who has hollowed the bones of the eyes?" (p. 81)

Not, however, that Watkins gives the last word to the Dead in this second movement, for when they see they have stricken terror into the Living, and made them put their hands together in prayer, they cunningly exhort each other to press their advantage in getting "one step nearer/The live coals in the grate," thereby betraying as base a desire for material comforts as the Living have displayed. As readers we are no more convinced by the arguments of the Dead than are the Living when the second movement closes.

In the final movement of the poem, driven by hunger and thirst, the Dead try one last desperate ploy: they concede everything that the Living want to believe about them. They admit they are evil, and they act evilly to substaniate their admission, uttering vicious curses to beat the cursing poems of the Welsh minstrels:

'God singe this doorway, hinge and bolt
If you keep our evil out.' (p. 83)

But when the Living still do not yield, the Dead again resort to their original pitch—an appeal to pity, but with a difference. They now speak to the question of the commonalty of humanity, saying, in effect: now you know our sins, we can clean the slate and make friends. After all, there is comfort in numbers, solidarity among sinners. Good divides, but evil unites. You Living are just as much a part of that great fraternity of vice—the Cains, the Delilahs, and the Barabbases—as are we the Dead:

'Know you are one with Cain the farm
And Dai of Dowlais pit;
You have thieved with Benjamin's robber's arm;

129

> With Delilah you lay by night.
> You cheated death with Barabbas the Cross
> When the dice of Hell came down.
> You prayed with Jo in the prisoners' fosse
> And ran about Rahab's town.' (p. 85)

In short, the Dead are turning back on the Living the names they have been called—lecher, gambler, murderer, thief and drunkard—not in angry retaliation so much as to stress their communion with the Living. But when that does not move the Living, the Dead voice their resentment that they are required to be so much better that the Living to be received by them.

But the moment of conscience comes and goes, the climax is reached and the Living remain unpersuaded. There is nothing left for the Dead to do but upbraid the Living for their self-deception:

> 'O crouch and cringe by the bounding flame
> And close your eyelids fast.
> Out of the breath of the year we came.
> The breath of the year has passed.' (p. 85)

As a final warning, they adjure the Living in future to let the Mari in when she knocks, for the Mari, the sacred skull, is much more than she appears, being beyond the ravages of Time:

> 'The wits of a skull are far too great
> Being out of the hands of the clock,
> When Mari Lwyd knocks on the door,
> In charity answer that knock.' (p. 86)

Though the Dead cast one last long lingering, envious look over their shoulder at the ham, the goose, the fire and the beer, their final words are uttered in a fading chant reaffirming the nature of the Mari and the nature of the ritual they have just taken part in—the archetypal parrying of the Fire by the Night-frost, the attempted rapprochement of Living and Dead. Their explanation of their failure is given in terms of the rejection of the Mari, whose mysteries cannot be comprehended or tolerated by the Living:

130

'None can look out and bear that sight,
None can bear that shock,
The Mari's shadow is too bright,
Her brilliance is too black.
None can bear that terror
When the pendulum swings back
Of the stiff and stuffed and stifled thing
Gleaming in the sack.' (p. 87)

And once again, despite all the games they have played, all the lies they have told, we find the truth in them.

Authorial Values

There is a third perspective in the poem, a neutral perspective, which carries the norms, the authorial position. At the beginning this view is expressed by the Announcer of the Ballad, who recites the Prologue. There, the return of the Dead is stated as a fact, a "given" of the action, so that there can be no question of dream or hallucination or charade or fancy dress. We are told that the Living have cast out the Dead, made them Exiles; and that their motivation is "their own fear of themselves." Yet despite this attempt by the Living to deny that the Dead exist, says the Announcer, they cannot blot out the sound of the Dead tapping at the panes, though they try to neutralize their terror with scorn and by huddling around the fire. By denying the Dead, says the Announcer, the Living suffer loneliness and "singleness of heart"—a term which is used in the Acts of the Apostles (2.46) to describe the clearness of purpose of the saved and baptized who spend their time in community and communion, but is used here perjoratively, being by implication identified with single-mindedness, closed-mindedness, estrangement and isolation.

A number of undesignated stanzas at the beginning of the Ballad proper, presumably to be spoken by the Announcer in a performed version of the Ballad, carry the anchor position as the action unfolds. These stanzas describe the Dead rising from their coffins—apparently glass-topped, as is sometimes the custom—and from their graves.

The agents for bringing the Dead to life in the Ballad, according to these preliminary stanzas, are the "terrible, picklock Charities." And who are these? Are they the Greek Charities, the three Graces, who shared an altar with Dionysus at Elis, and who, in the ancient mystery drama were the invokers of the sacred king (Graves, p. 326)? Certainly in the Ballad they are the openers of the door between the natural and the supernatural worlds, the ministrants—albeit somewhat grubby and sneaky and sinister—who try to effect union between the inhabitants of this world and the Other. Recalling superstitions in which rodents are messengers between the living and the dead, Watkins's Charities gnaw beneath the walls of the Living, like ferrets, burrowing into graves and resurrecting the Dead.

Lending support to the mediating role of the Charities is the mention of the Eucharistic objects of Chalice and Wafer in the first of the couplet refrains, which also carry the neutral view between the Living and the Dead:

> Chalice and Wafer. Wine and Bread.
> And the picklock, picklock, picklock, tread.   (p. 70)

As we have already noted above when the Dead employed the expression "breaking of bread," they obviously saw the sacramental implications of the "moment of conscience." Now we see that the neutral narrator and chorus apparently share this view. Watkins's stage directions at the beginning of the Ballad proper, seems to highlight this implication:

(Pitchblack Darkness—A Long Table laid with a White Cloth. . . . . The Two loads of a Pendulum. . . . A Skull may be suggested at one shadow-limit of the Pendulum, and a Fillet at the other.)   (p. 70)

Perhaps the capitalization in this stage direction is intended to invest the scene with solemn importance, perhaps even to suggest the symbolism of an altar. The swing of the pendulum between the symbols of death and life suggest mediation. Just as at the ritual breaking of bread and drinking of wine of the Christian Eucharist union is effected between the celebrant and his God, so Watkins may be conceiving of a similar union at the joint or hinge of the old and new years.

That this symbolic Communion Table and the Charities are indeed the place and agency for a divine visitation is further suggested by another stanza in this beginning sequence by the neutral narrator, when he speaks of experiencing the awesome phenomenon of:

> The breath of a numb thing, loud and faint:
> Something found and lost.   (p. 71)

and asks:

> What mounted, murderous thing goes past
> The room of Pentecost?

Now these allusions suggest that the New Year's Eve celebration is to be equated with the occasion described in Acts 2, 1-4. In the room where the Apostles sat, seven weeks after Christ's Easter resurrection, came a sudden sound from Heaven and a mighty rushing wind followed by cloven tongues of fire which sat on each of them. If Pentecost (White Sunday) was the time of the visitation of the Christian Holy Ghost, might not the turning of the year in the House of the Living be the time and place for the visitation of the White Spirit, the pagan ghost of the Mari Lwyd—the "Mounted, murderous thing" passing at that moment? Certainly the visitation of the Mari is accompanied by similar mysteries and wonders as was the descent of the Holy Ghost, and she certainly evokes the same terrible awe. Moreover, if she is indeed the White Goddess, she has the inspirational power comparable to that of the Holy Ghost to make sons and daughters prophesy, young men see visions, and old men dream dreams (Acts 2.17).

It is interesting to note here that Frazer found that "the function originally assigned to the Holy Spirit may have been that of the divine mother."[4] Frazer points out that in the apocryphal *Gospel to the Hebrews,* Christ spoke of the Holy Ghost as his mother. The passage, quoted by Origen (*Comment in Joan.* II, vol. iv, col. 132, ed. Migne) runs: "My mother the Holy Spirit took me a moment ago by one of my hairs and carried me away to the great Mount Tabor." Frazer also notes that the Ophites

---

4 *The Dying God* (London, 1923), being Vol. 4 of *The Golden Bough,* p. 5, n.3.

represented the Holy Spirit as "the first woman," "mother of all living." This time the fusion in the Ballad of the White Ghost of the Mari with Mary-cum-Holy Ghost carries the full authority of the neutral narrator.

We should also remind ourselves here again that the ceremony of wine and bread was a fundamental part of the ritual evocation of the Earth Mother in many of her aspects. Certainly we should also note again the equation of the Cauldron of Inspiration with the Holy Grail, and consider if these reverberations are valid for the Chalice and Wafer of the Ballad.

The descent and indwelling of the Holy Spirit, such as was experienced by the Apostles, brings man Grace or *Caritas,* from the Greek *Kharis,* grace, favour, which gives us the words both Grace and Charity. Through such a visitation are the spiritual desires of the practising Christian satisfied, and his guilt cleansed. Is the White Spirit of the Mari Lwyd meant to bring similar benefits to the Living in the Ballad?

To answer this we need to look further at the function of the Dead in the Ballad as revealed in the statements by the neutral narrator and the chorus. The well-behaved corpses, so straight and stiff and tidy in their white-sheet shrouds, *do* return as "heretic, drunkard and thief" as the Living claim, but only because they return as they were in life, no better and no worse. When the narrator says that "good men gone are evil become" he is not suggesting that the Dead have become evil in *fact.* The change has occurred primarily in the attitude of the Living, who have forgotten that—as the early Celt believed—the dead always continue as they were while living, no better, no worse, a mixture of the usual assortment of strengths and weaknesses. If the Dead in the poem do appear malign in their urgency to make contact, the narrator suggests, it is only because the Living forgot them the moment they clamped them down, for, again according to ancient Celtic belief, the Dead become restless and threatening only if their continuing needs are neglected:

> Good men gone are evil become
> And the men that you nailed down

134

Clamped in darkness, clamour for rum,
And ravish on beds of down
The vision your light denied them, laid
Above the neglected door;   (p. 71)

At the beginning of the second movement of the poem, the neutral narrator, now designated "Voice," again stresses the similarity between the Dead and the Living. The terror in the situation is not on account of any especially sinister nature of the Dead, but implicit in the high solemnity of the moment, which, if celebrated to its fullest, would bring about the confrontation of Living and Dead.

Quietness stretches the pendulum's chain
To the limit where terrors start,
Where the dead and the living find again
They beat with the selfsame heart.   (p. 77)

Again between the second and third movements the mixed nature of the Dead, their essential humanness, like the Living, is stressed by the neutral Voice:

Dread and quiet, evil and good:
Frost in the night has mixed their blood.

Thieving and giving, good and evil:
The beggar's a saint, and the saint a devil . . .   (p. 82)

Clearly, then, it was Watkins's intention to give equal force and favour to the Dead as to the Living as far as their respective natures were concerned. He wished only to unite them at the crack of the year, to have them accept each other for what they were, and thus to forgive each other, as the closing statement of his after-note makes clear:

I have attempted to bring together those who are separated. The last breath of the year is their threshold, the moment of supreme forgiveness, confusion and understanding, the profane and sacred moment impossible to realise while the clock hands divide the Living from the Dead. (p. 89)

For, as he notes in his essay on the "New Year, 1965", in that "eternal moment of contradictions" the miracle of a "reconciliation of contraries" is possible.

So what is the evocation of the Dead and of the White Spirit of the Mari by the Charities intended to do for the Living? To create in them through communion with the Dead some kind of epiphany which will fulfill and enrich them, apparently. Which is not to say that Watkins meant us to seize this myth on its literal level only. The Mari and the Contenders of the Quick and the Dead invite allegoric and angogic interpretation—in the mediaeval sense of "allegory," which is but to say that the myth symbolizes more than its "face."[5] Though the levels beyond the literal are not those spiritual and mystical levels in the sense employed in mediaeval exegesis, they are philosophical and psychological levels of relevance to the modern world.

Rendering these mythical and religious terms into psychological ones, might we not say that the ferreting Charities represent an uneasy, perhaps unwelcome, but compelling impulse for honesty in man, for the letting of understanding enter into him, despite his preference to remain ignorant and uninvolved? To put it another way, might not the grave-opening, secret-exposing Charities represent the quest for self-knowledge which the surrender of prejudice and the cultivation of humility might make possible? Then the spiritual communion of Living and Dead, and the epiphany of the Mari, might be understood as awareness, insight, vision, open-mindedness, especially illumination at those moments of heightened sensitivity.

The pity of it is that in the Ballad the Living fail to surrender to the moment, fail to aspire to the supreme forgiveness which is like the shock of the spark as Dead and Living meet. Unlike the Apostles at Pentecost, they do not permit themselves to be filled with something akin to the Holy Spirit. They have not "in charity" let the Mari in. Instead:

> Betrayed are the living, betrayed the dead:
> All are confused by a horse's head.   (p. 82)

5 Since this study was completed, I have written an essay on the marked affinity of Watkins's vision to mediaeval meditational and allegorical modes: "Gateways to the Vision of Vernon Watkins," *The Anglo-Welsh Review*, XX, No. 45 (1971), 131-140.

If *we* are equally confused about the conflicting claims of Living and Dead, the Voice sets us straight: the Mari *is* "a sacred thing" that the Dead carry through the night, notwithstanding the constant refrain that the horse's head in the frost is both sinner and saint—for, after all, the Earth Mother is both maker and breaker of life, emblem of life and death. And, as the final movement draws to a close, when the hands of the clock have passed the moment of midnight, when the Dead, with one last longing look at the feast, are beginning to stiffen back into death, as rigid as the midnight-straight hands of the clock, when, in short, it is too late for the moment of community of living and dead to be achieved, the Living are told that they have indeed been in the presence of the divine, even though the god was in the guise of a beggar:

> Eyes on the cloth. Eyes on the plate.
> Rigor mortis straightens the figure.
> Striking the clock when the hands are straight,
> You have seen a god in the eyes of a beggar.   (p. 87)

If there are readers who are shocked by Watkins's merging of Christian elements such as the Eucharistic appointments of cloth and plate with the pagan feast, and the descent of the Holy Spirit with the visitation of the Mari, it could be because they suffer the same tunnel vision as the Living of the Ballad, or because they misunderstand what Watkins was about. Surely Watkins, a sincere Anglican, had no intention of demoting Christian faith any more than of extolling pagan rites. Myth and doctrines are blended within the boundaries of the poem to produce a vehicle whose tenor is religious in both a more complex and more elemental way. Graves has commented on a similar need to range widely over past and present belief and symbol to convey his own metaphysical position:

> Poets who are concerned with the single poetic Theme cannot afford to draw disingenuous distinction between "sacred history" and "profane myth" and make the usual dissociation between them, unless prepared to reject the Scriptures as wholly irrelevant to poetry. This would be a pity, and in these days of religious toleration I cannot see why they need accept so glaringly unhistorical a view of the authorship, provenience, dating and ori-

ginal texts of the Old Testament, that its close connexion with the Theme is severed. (p. 314)

Watkins's position in the Ballad would seem to be that he regrets the stance of his contemporaries, the Living, who, blatant materialists, paying only lip service to the Christian faith, have turned their backs on the past, who feel no historical, cultural or metaphysical affinity with those who have gone before, and who thereby deny the relevance of the constantly renewing cycle of life, the community of all creation through all time. Watkins does not specifically promote or defend the Mari *per se,* but uses her as a symbol of the hopes, desires, and fears of those long dead, as well as suggesting her affinity with other symbols on which men in different times right up to the present have focussed. By concentration on that symbol, the dead for whom the symbol had meaning can be resurrected—at least in the imagination and understanding of the open-minded, the aware. The Mari and the Dead may best be understood on the symbolic level as our cultural and spiritual roots which the wise hold constantly in mind. The turning of the year is the traditional time to look back and to look forward, and for a single instant, to distill in our imagination all of time, of history and the future, in a single harmony. The imagination does now what primitive people once thought to occur literally: the Dead *do* walk, the god *does* appear, and they *do* have communion with the Living. The pivot of the year, charged in all cultures of all time with such high significance, becomes a moment of *anamnesis,* or recollection and reappraisal, the psychological equivalent of a religious sacrament or of celebration of a mystery to call down the diety, a visitation by a holy spirit. At its best such recollection encompasses all that man has felt and believed from the Paleolithic "Red Lady" and the "fossil-man asleep in the ground" up to the "man on the top of Dover cliff" or any other men alive.[6] The myths themselves will have relevance if only for purposes of comparison and contrast in the re-evaluation of our own faith, but of still more importance is the sense of perpetuity of humanity, and

6 See Watkins's "Ballad of the Rough Sea," in *The Death Bell,* p. 69.

immortality of man-ness, if not of man, that we experience in this stock-taking.

In "New Year, 1965" Watkins states some of these thoughts in another way. He sees the year as a ring of time, whose unity, however, cannot be seen as we travel through it, just as one cannot see the satisfying expanse of a sea "containing all its contradictions, all its opposing forces, in a single harmonious vision," while one is travelling across it. By implication, the moment the year is completed we can see it as a harmonious whole, a circle, so that in that vital moment hovering at midnight of New Year's Eve, we can bring it all together in a way that we cannot while we are travelling through time and history.

It is such a mystic moment when the past is seized in the present with vividness and immediacy that Watkins celebrates in "The Turning of the Stars" (*The Death Bell*, pp. 23-25):

> There is a moment when Apollo's tree
> Is Daphne still. The Past is not the Past
> But wound within a ring
> So finely wrought,
> It knows each path and avenue of thought.
> Downward he looks, through heaven and earth, to see
> The sunlight and dayspring
> Caught in her eyes, all uttered love surpassed
> By that first heaven which knows her timelessly.

Such a moment is one of illumination, of epiphany, wherein a touch "the pivot of the god/Like light revealed."

To achieve such a moment of harmonious vision, Watkins continues in "New Year, 1965" (p. 22), we have paradoxically to keep travelling, and travelling away from it. The paradox is that resolution is only achieved by perpetual movement. Thus we cannot experience the supreme moment of resolution unless our minds and imaginations keep travelling over the past, and off into the future:

> It is true that if I am looking for the roots of a country I must turn my eyes away from that image of unity, resolved in its perpetual movement, the sea of dissolution and beginning, the serpent swallowing its own tail. I must look away even from that cave only a few miles from here where the oldest skeleton found in Britain was unearthed. . . . I must forget the perfect, unblemished mirror,

139

and see what man has made. It is necessary to dig up the past to understand the present.

Unearthed skeletons, Watkins reminds us, "trinkets and ornaments dug from Welsh clay," and archaeological finds generally, are not the only way to retrieve the past. Art can perform this function for us too, helping us "see all that had vigorous life in the past as contemporary with ourselves, and ourselves as falling away from that, if we do not correct our vision."

What happens at this falling away is what has happened to the Living of his Ballad: blindness, prejudice, self-deception, smugness, crass materialism, insensitivity, unawareness, take over. Watkins speaks in the same essay of Yeats's condemnation of the same deficiencies:

> He disliked what he called "mechanical apathy", which deadened a race and made people lose their awareness. Everything he valued was a miracle, and he particularly cherished those characters who exhibited a heroic attitude to life and death.

It was to warn against such a "falling away" into "mechanical apathy," and to help make up for the deficiency, that Watkins wrote his "Ballad of the Mari Lwyd." In chosing a horse's skull as "the image of the Old Year," "the image of New Year's Eve"—themselves microcosms of the past stretching all the way back to the man in the Paviland Cave—he was trying to lead the Living, his own contemporaries, to the miracle of a happier New Year, by making them aware of "the eternal companionship of the past in the present."[7]

7 Roland Mathias, "A Note on Some Recent Poems by Vernon Watkins," *Dock Leaves,* I, No. 3 (1950), 43 ff.

CHAPTER VII

THE THEME OF THE PAST IN OTHER
POEMS IN THE CANON

Watkins's concern with the merging of the past into present awareness is reflected throughout the canon. The variations are many, bespeaking Watkins's constant preoccupation with the central question of time.

The Past as Supernatural in the Other Ballads

As in the "Ballad of the Mari Lwyd," Watkins's other ballads also tend to deal with the theme of the past in terms of supernatural communication between the Living and the Dead, appropriately so since the supernatural has always been an important element in ballad tradition. It is significant that a number of these ballads occur in the volume titled *The Death Bell*.

In the "Ballad of Hunt's Bay" (*The Death Bell*, pp. 84-88), a black stick washed up by the sea becomes a "divining-rod" which puts the poet in touch with the past and with the drowned sailors of the foundered timbers from which the stick has come. The "haunting host" of the ghosts of the dead in sackcloth speak through "the floating wood and the breath inside," which is "the breath of the god," even though logic scoffs:

> How can a voice come out of a sack
> Or breath from pieces of wood gone black?

But a deeper knowledge countermands:

> Spirit laid in the long dumb wood,
> . . . .

141

> Rise till you come where men are cast
> To a music binding Future and Past
> Heard by Ulysses, lashed to the mast.

The music, is, of course, the life stuff, reservoir of light and love in the bosom of the Earth Mother,[1] as we have remarked in the mare and foal poems and the "Music of Colour" poems above.

In the "Ballad of the Equinox" (*The Death Bell,* pp. 72-74), the same stick, "though itself a barren thing," mediates past and present, this world and the Other, for "it has been where none has been." This poem celebrates Pwlldu (Welsh for "black pool"). The spot itself is below the cliffs of the coast of Gower just west of Bishopton valley—Pwlldu Bay and Pwlldu Head belonging to the National Trust. Accommodating its pastness into its presentness, Watkins knows it as "an eternal place" where

> The black stream under the stones
> Carries the bones of the dead,
> The starved, the talkative bones.

Meditation on these dead and this eternal sea permits the tormented individual to surmount the problem and moods of the moment, for the former are real, the latter "theatrical," mere "allegorical shadow" of the true. Such a Platonic devaluation of the existent, however, is not a characteristic position of Watkins as we shall see below.

In other ballads, the dead themselves return. In the "Ballad of the Rough Sea" (*The Death Bell,* pp. 69-71), "a fossil-man in his bed of chalk" who "turned in his grave and began to talk" stood up in the rock to meet the man on the top of the cliff and observe the drama of fishermen on a sea so rough it is "white as a shroud . . . whiter than whitest moon or cloud."

---

1 Let us note that Graves asserts that the Sirens were a triad or ennead of orgiastic moon-priestesses, born of one of the Muses, or in competition with them (p. 418); certainly some manifestation of the Great Goddess in her attenuated phase.

The Personal Past and Nostalgia

The past which Watkins would have us merge into present awareness includes the individual's personal memories and history, as well as a sense of man's generic antecedents. Continuing consciousness of one's personal past should not, however, be any mere sentimental dwelling on memories—regrets, nostalgia, remorse—at the expense of a full life in the present.

The poem "Returning to Goleufryn" (*The Lady with the Unicorn,* pp. 15-16) is woven out of highly personal memories. He returns—and he uses the imagery of the prodigal son, though it is the town he calls "prodigal"—to the home of his grandfather in Carmarthen on the River Towy, one of the few rivers on which the primitive boat, the coracle, is still used for salmon fishing under jealously-guarded privileges handed down from father to son. The place is so evocative of the vivid memories of childhood, he likens it to "a book of the Psalms" shut "on the leaves and pressed flowers of a journey." The present in the poem is conveyed in a series of tremulous, translucent images of house and garden:

> All is sunny
> In the garden behind you. The soil is alive with
> blind-petalled blooms
> Plundered by bees. Gooseberries and currants are gay
> With tranquil, unsettled light.

The present is intermingled with flashes of the past:

> O lead me that I may drown
> In those earlier cobbles, reflected; a street that is
> strewn with palms
> Rustling with blouses and velvet.

Yet even as he loses himself in the warmth and order of the house and garden of other days, he feels another kind of lostness. To wish himself back in the past would involve a denial of all those he has known since he was a child, which, in turn, would involve a betrayal of the past, of the house which symbolizes all of the values of his childhood, and this he will not do:

> I shall not unnumber one soul I have stood with
> and known
> To regain your stars struck by horses, your sons of God
> breaking in song.

Remembrance of the past, constant awareness of our roots, is essential to full consciousness. But not, the poet reminds us, in the sense of wallowing in memory. A yearning to recapture the pleasure of seeing a horse's shoe strike sparks as it hits the road, a longing to feel again that first moving experience of hearing Welsh hymns sung in chapel, can be as destructive of the full life as a total fixation on the present. Nostalgic denial of the present is as undesirable as denial of the past. Integration of actuality and memory is the optimum condition.

This is the sense of the pair of poems "Fidelity to the Dead" and "Fidelity to the Living" (*The Lady with the Unicorn*, p. 40). Watkins turns from contemplation, in the first poem, of the dead whom "Immortal silence transfigures," and whose love and light teach him not to "fear what the blind Fate weaves," back to the living in the second poem, realizing that too deep a concentration on the past and on death does a disservice to life. "Tenuous life, I have wronged you," here recalls the question asked when he lost himself in memories in his grandfather's house" "Which way would I do you wrong?" The resolution lies in the realization that the very tenuousness of life is light and joy—which death merely holds in secret awaiting the time of regeneration. Thus are we all joined, living to living, living to dead, by the spun thread—the image woven all the way through this pair of poems. Though this thread puts us in mind of the thread played out and cut by the Fates or Norns, emanations in triad, as we have seen, of the Great Goddess, the thread in Watkins's vision is associated with more than the destiny of the individual. Incorporated in the image is the notion of the life stuff out of which life is spun and woven time and time again, "the very thread which binds" mother to child and leaf to leaf.

The Past and Idealism

This sense of pastness cultivated by the fully-functioning consciousness is no mere historic sense any more than it is sentimental nostalgia. As intimated in the commentary on Watkins's poems the individual and time as a span from past into future represents the individual genus. The present, actual, literal, naturalistic mare and foal are apprehended simultaneously with the generic mare and foal — the concept of enduring mareness and foalness. It is this notion of the perpetuity of life implicit in the transient existence of the particular creature which constitutes the sense of pastness (and futurity) that Watkins clearly possesses, and would have his Living in the "Ballad of the Mari Lwyd" possess.

The quality of generic continuity may be seized, perhaps, as a sort of Idealism mediating Plato and Aristotle. The generic or mythic mare (or foal) is a form never seen in nature, of which the particular, natural mare (or foal) seems but a copy; yet it is apprehended by man's capacity to remember, think (thus, abstract and generalize), and imagine, and exists in that very real sense. We begin to see, then, that the "Idealism" of the group of poems called "Music of Colours," is not purely Platonic, for pure white, "original" white, true white, *is* accessible to man, is *not* something belonging to an inaccessible world of Forms.

But our experience of white is not something direct and immediate. We perceive it, Watkins shows us in "Music of Colours Dragonfoil and the Furnace of Colours" (*Affinities,* pp. 80-83), in the brilliant variety of flowers and creatures "sprung from the white fire," "nurtured of the white light," "breaking from the white bones/Snows never seen." For the secret music of light and life and ideal time "is for us transfigured into colours," of which imperfect white is one:

> Bright petal, dragonfoil, springing from the hot grass,
> Dazzling profusion continually fading,
> Sprung from the white fire, tiger-lily, snake-fang
> Basking in brilliance; deep in fume of poppies
> Sleep the black stamens.

Where were these born then, nurtured of the white light?
Dragonfly, kingfisher breaking from the white bones,
Snows never seen, nor blackthorn boughs in winter,
Lit by what brand of a perpetual summer,
These and the field flowers?

This original whiteness is perceived and perpetuated, too, in the rainbow of the spray:

Far off, continually, I can hear the breakers
Falling, destroying, secret, while the rainbow,
Flying in spray, perpetuates the white light,
Ocean, kindler of us, mover and mother,
Constantly changing.

Only in the "continually fading" process of the flowers, and the "continually . . . falling, destroying," action of the breakers is the white light perceptible in the rainbow of colours. For this is the paradox: true white and the light of perpetual summer can be glimpsed and apprehended only in vitality subject to decay.

This is the force of the Eurydice/Orpheus myth interwoven in the poem. This myth was a retelling in Thrace of the seasonal myth, Orpheus being son of Calliope (one of the Muses, a nine-fold manifestation of the Great Goddess), and thus the star son or sacred King as substantiated by his orgiastic dismemberment celebrated in mysteries named for him. The seasonal myth emphasizes at one and the same time the transience of nature and the perpetuation of life through the miracle of regeneration. Music, the life stuff, the thread of light in Watkins's symbolism, was divinity made manifest in Thracian legend. Only when Eurydice went to the Underworld did Orpheus play his moving music. It is by virtue of the flowers continually fading, the breakers continually breaking and destroying, the seasons changing, Eurydice leaving, that Light, Love, Pure White, Music, can be apprehended by us. "Only by absence is the song made/Audible":

June wakes the music that was known to Orpheus,
Breathed by the fire-god, muted for enchantment,
Fire-misted marigold, clustered myosotis
Sprung to remember the river's lamentation,
June flowers hiding the footprints of Eurydice
Seized by the dark king.

146

Yet the turf tells me: she it is, no other,
Touches the rose-blaze, gathers what became her
Music. Forgetfulness holds her like a girdle
Silent. Only by absence is the song made
Audible. Orpheus, leaving above Lethe,
Knows every note there.

Just as music apprehended by the senses is Divine Music incarnated, so is the "perennial wonder" of the blaze of summer colors "the sudden incarnation" of Pure, Eternal White—a sudden incarnation which is "True for this moment, therefore never dying." For the principle of continuity is ever implicit in change and decay. The black stamens sleep in the heart of the blossom, carrying the life stuff, the white light, for the following season.

Paradoxically, however, while Watkins tells how the Ideal is experienced and perpetuated through the natural and transient, and while he weaves a poem magic enough to give us a glimpse of the blinding luminescence of Original White, he uses the vocabulary of Platonic Idealism—"patterns," "shadows" of another world as in the Allegory of the Cave, and other words and phrases from the doctrine of Recollection:

There the stream flies on to its own beginning,
Slips through the fresh banks, woods of their escaping,
Leaving in glory patterns of a lost world,
Leaves that are shadows of a different order,
Light, born of white light, broken by the wave's plunge
Here into colours.

And:

All that is made here hides another making;
Even this water shows a magic surface.
Sky is translated; dragonfly and iris
Rise from the grey sheath; unremembered shadows
Cling, where the bloom breaks.

. . . .

Waking entranced, we cannot see that other
Order of colours moving in the white light.
Time is for us transfigured into colours
Known and remembered from an earlier summer,
Or into breakers.

The same theme of the Ideal apprehended in the phenomenal is treated in "The Immortal in Nature" (*Cypress and Acacia,* p. 53). The first stanza introduces the same symbolic equation of Music equals Light equals White equals Love or Life, absolutes perpetuated and seized only in the fleeting phenomena of nature:

> I must forget these things, and yet lose none.
> Music is light, and shadows all are they.
> White is the fountain that begot the sun.
> Light on the petal falls; then falls the may.

What are "these things" of the first line? Natural things, things that pass away. Why must they be forgotten? "Must" does not express compulsion here, but certainty: the poet is bound to forget what is so transitory, so ephemeral. Yet he should not, or would not, lose them, in the sense that he must distill from them what represents the noumenon or the enduring essence of them.

Again Watkins uses Platonic vocabulary: these transient phenomena are but shadows of the light that is music—the divine life stuff. White (pure, original white) is another name for the same stuff. It was the colour of the fountain (another name for music-light-life) which made the sun. This essential ingredient makes the petal, and lights up that petal of may-blossom, which is here a symbol for all that decays and dies.

So what is immortal in nature? These components and manifestations of the life material out of which individual existences are spun, whose threads are all there are by which to know this never-depleted reservoir (source, fountain) of music (light, love) held secretly in the inscrutable blackness of the womb of earth (vase, pitcher, hill).

If the Ideal can be seized through the natural which partakes of the transcendent, how can the qualities of timelessness and spacelessness, or ubiquity, be seized? If the imperfectly white hawthorn blossom bodies forth true (Real) white, can its very transient life embody eternity? Watkins answers that memory provides the sense of continuity, and his first line is further illuminated. Though we forget the particular bloom, we do not lose the essence of blossomness; though lovers pass away or part, we remember love:

> I tell my soul: Although they be withdrawn,
> Meditate on those lovers. Think of Donne
> Who could contract all ages to one day,
> Knowing they were but copies of that one:
> The first being true, then none can pass away.

Through memory and imagination the mind of man can con-
tract eternity into a single day, as Donne did. Knowing one day
well, he could know what all the other days that go to make up
the ages must be like. Though Watkins again uses Platonic
vocabulary—"copies of that one"—he is not suggesting that
each day is a copy of some unknown, unexperienced Ideal;
rather that the "Ideal" day is the one that is so richly experienced that the imagination can project it into an eternity by
conceiving of an infinity of copies of the "Ideal" experience. In
this poem it would seem that Watkins's Idealism is existential!
The lines: "True for this moment, therefore never dying," in
"Music of Colours—Dragonfoil . . ." and "The first being true,
then none can pass away," in "The Immortal in Nature," beautifully express the notion of experience of the transient preced-
ing the apprehension of essential forms.

Then Watkins hits the paradox which is the crux of an
existential apprehension of Ideality: there can be no beauty
approximating the ideal without time and its corollary decay.
In "Sunday Morning" Wallace Stevens stated the paradox:
"Death is the Mother of Beauty." Watkins puts it this way:

> Where time is not, all nature is undone,
> For nature grows in grandeur of decay.
> These royal colours that the leaves put on
> Mark the year living in his kingly way;
> Yet, when he dies, not he but time is gone.

What is more, music and light—the immortal material of
life—emerge from perishable man, from artists like Beeth-
oven, Milton, Michelangelo, who produce immortal forms
from nature's ephemerae:

> Beethoven's music nature could not stun.
> Light rushed from Milton.
> See the Sistine ray.

149

There burns the form eternally begun.
That soul whose very hand made marble pray,
The untempted, mightiest master, holds in sway
The wrestling sinews death had seemed to own
And might have owned, but that they were not clay.

In "The Replica" (*Cypress and Acacia,* pp. 87-88), Watkins
again refashions Idealism out of his own unique vision, and
again employs Platonic and Neo-Platonic terminology in an
original way. The term "replica" occurs in all occult thinking
stemming from the basic Chaldean belief that the world is a
replica of heaven, and that everything that exists in perfect form
in the latter place, has its replica or reflection in the other.[2] But
it would be a disasterous error to take it for granted that
Watkins was using the word with metaphysical connotations.
In fact, the first lines clue us in to a novel definition at work:

Once more the perfect pattern falls asleep,
And in the dark of sleep the replica
Springs to awareness.

Taking the image of the foal which Watkins supplies in the
continuing context—

Light is born of dark
As the young foal beside his mother steps,
Closer than her own shadow.

—we see that each particular foal that dies constitutes a
"pattern," a model, a thing to be copied or imitated, while each
particular foal that is born, made of light, born into light, out of
the buried light in the inscrutable blackness, constitutes a
"replica," a copy or imitation of the pattern. The new-born foal
will himself, at the completion of his life cycle, fall asleep as "the
perfect pattern" presumably, having meanwhile borne a foal in
replica to continue the process.

This is indeed a very strange kind of "Idealism" in which the
Ideal Form—the perfect pattern—and the shadow or
copy—the replica—co-exist indivisibly in the same entity. And
yet this is exactly the way Watkins sees it. Even in a patently

2 John Senior, *The Way Down and Out: The Occult in Symbolist Literature*
(Cornell U. P., Ithaca, New York, 1959), p. 11.

Christian context, as in "The Conception" (*The Lady with the Unicorn,* p. 70), the child conceived is called a "sacred pattern, leaping from time's loom," and it is the mother's body which contains "the ordained tranquility of forms." Natural phenomena again partake of the immortal and ideal by being pattern as well as replica.

In the world of creatures, the replica perpetuates the pattern. Like the blue and white foals in "Foal," each being is on the one hand unique and temporal; on the other generic and immortal. So, in "The Replica," Watkins used the analogy of the waterfall to elucidate this mystery. Just as "the waterfall by falling is renewed/And still is falling," so are the changing "replicas" of man and beast perpetuating the unchanging, perfect pattern. The central paradox of creaturely life, as of the tree and of the waterfall, is that constancy is always apprehended in change:

> All its countless changes
> Accumulate to nothing but itself.
> . . . .
> We know it lives by being consumed, we know
> Its voice is new and ancient, and its force
> Flies from a single impulse that believes
> Nothing is vain, though all is cast for sorrow.

This duality of ideal and actual as experienced in the waterfall is also applied to the brook in "Bishopston Stream" *(Affinities,* p. 71). There the water has two voices, one of darkness, symbolic of all time and perpetual life, one of day and the present and of beautiful transience. Always against the sound of the latter "there is a second river/Speaks by its silence," an eternal water that has flowed throughout time.

Watkins does not suggest that this "second river" exists in some other dimension, as, say a Platonic Ideal Form. Rather, it seems to be compounded solely out of the memory—personal and historic—and the imagination of man, a compound of recollected experience. In fact, in "Ode.to the Spring Equinox" *(Cypres and Acacia,* pp. 96-99), Watkins seems to elevate the particular, contingent and actual, the "passing moment," over all abstractions and absolutes:

151

> I watch, and feel the pulse of turning Earth
> Now, in the forespring time,
> And mark that power sublime
> Which makes the passing moment worth
> All unformed years lacking this present form.

The "power sublime"—so reminiscent of Wordsworth's "a sense sublime/Of something far more deeply interfused," in "Tintern Abbey"—is that which is felt in the present and actual alone, presumably.

To the extent that the immortal, supernal, or eternal are valid concepts, Watkins did not care to locate them as the Platonist or orthodox Christian might do. Such questions cannot be answered in objective, logical terms. So, in "The Replica" he says:

> If you ask
> Where may divinity or love find rest
> When all moves forward to a new beginning
> And each obeys one constant law of change,
> I cannot answer.

Yet Watkins does suggest an answer: it is given to man to know that though life obeys the law of change, in every fresh birth, every replica of love, "time is overthrown":

> Yet to man alone,
> Moving in time, birth gives a timeless movement
> To taste the secret of the honeycomb
> And pluck from night that blessing which outweighs
> All the calamities and griefs of time.
> There shines the one scene worthy of his tears,
> For in that dark the greatest light was born
> Which, if man sees, then time is overthrown,
> And afterwards all acts are qualified
> By knowledge of that interval of glory:
> Music from heaven, the incomparable gift
> Of God to man, in every infant's eyes
> That vision which is ichor to the soul
> Transmitted there by lightning majesty,
> The replica, reborn, of Christian love.

Although the poem ends on a Christian note, there is no notion of either a paradise of eternal forms, or of perpetuation of man through the Christian concept of life after death. As in Marianne Moore's poem "What Are Years?" and Wallace Stevens's "Sunday Morning," eternity is in mortality.

CHAPTER VIII

THE POET'S ROLE IN RECOVERY AND
PRESERVATION OF THE PAST

If awareness of the past—which gives insight into life's continuity and into the way constancy inheres in change—is vital to
the full-functioning of the human spirit, how may this vision be
conveyed to those like the Living in the "Ballad of the Mari
Lwyd," who so desperately need it?

That is the business of the poet. What makes him a poet is his
capacity to integrate all that is past into the present moment. In
effect he possesses the gift of the shaman to negotiate time and
space. "All good artists have something ancient about them,"
Watkins says in "New Year, 1965," elaborating:

> So far as time is concerned, I think poets and artists differ from so
> many others in that their consciousness and will move upstream
> rather than down. Their eyes are directed to the source rather than
> to the estuary, so they see all that had vigorous life in the past as
> contemporary with ourselves.

In those poems where Watkins has written of the nature and
function of the poet, this gift is often expressed as communion
with the dead, comparable to the experience that the Dead and
Living were supposed to achieve in the "Ballad of the Mari
Lwyd." Of "The Poets in Whom Truth Lives" (*Cypress and
Acacia,* pp. 18-19) he says:

> Lives of the dead you share,
> Earth-hid in tender trust.

Being one of that group, he comments on his own experience in
"The Mask of Winter" (*Cypress and Acacia,* pp. 75-76):

153

> I cannot separate,
> So soundlessly they shine,
> The windings of past fate,
> Nor the lost lives from mine.

Surely Watkins did not mean us to take this communion with the dead literally, any more than he meant us to take it literally in the "Ballad of the Mari Lwyd." Nor could he have wanted us to understand his impulse as a conventionally elegiac one. Our study of the Ballad has pointed to the fact that the old Celtic belief of communion between dead and living is serving as a metaphor for the poet's role of contracting the past into the present. With his orphic lyre, he overturns death and time, unites birth and death, and reconciles contradictions in paradoxes:

> Time that is over
> Comes not again;
> Yet instinctive
> The strings remain.
> All is fugitive,
> Nothing vain.
>
> Magical foliage
> Glittering shone.
> There they trembled
> Who now are gone.
> Dancers perish:
> The dance goes on.
>
>> "Touch with Your Fingers"
>> (*Cypress and Acacia,* pp. 77-78)

What is the nature of the poet's power that he can do this? He is privileged to possess some of the special life stuff—love, light music—out of which new forms are generated. What the poet creates with that life stuff is art. By participating in creation—as we are shown in "Buried Light" (*Cypress and Acacia,* p. 82)—the poet partakes of divinity:

> Come, buried light, and honour time
> With your dear gift, your constancy,
> That the known world be made sublime
> Through visions that closed eyelids see.

The poet's vision, in other words, is not natural vision alone; the light he "sees" by is not natural light. His is the vision of seer, or prophet or priest, or Sibyl, who has

> . . . . . the power to see what's gone
> So clearly, that what is or is to be
> Hinders no whit the noblest I have known . . ."
>
> "The Sibyl"
> (*Fidelities*, p. 13)

Where does this power of the poet come from? Like Graves, who called the poet's imaginative leap in time, or suspension of time, "proleptic" thought (p. 34), Watkins knows his source, his spring, his fountain to be the Muse. In "Demands of the Muse" (*Affinities*, p. 21), she says of her son/protégé/poet:

> Born into time of love's perceptions, he
> Is not of time. The acts of time to him
> Are marginal. From the first hour he knows me
> Until the last, he shall divine my words.
> In his own solitude he hears another.

Again from our study of the "Ballad of the Mari Lwyd" we may be sure that the myth is serving as a metaphor for the poetic process, and we already know what the myth is. Watkins's Muse is one with the Mari Lwyd, who is "out of the hands of the clock," and "knows all from the birth of the Flood/To this moment where we stand." The following claim from "Muse, Poet and Fountain" (*Affinities*, p. 24) leaves no doubt of this:

> Though time still falls from future into past,
> Nothing is gone my hand may not restore.
> Mine is the pulse that makes your pulse beat fast,
> Harmonious joy with stillness at the core.

The beat of the pulse puts us in mind of the inexorable ticking of the clock in the Ballad, and the "stillness at the core" reminds us of the still point at the joint of the years as the New Year arrives.

Casting light on the poems in the canon which have to do with the powers of the poet is the relationship, explored previously, between the Mari and Cerridwen, the Welsh Muse (before her attenuation into nine little departmental goddesses, as Graves puts it), with her Cauldron of Inspiration, the Awen.

155

As we saw in our study of the "Ballad of the Mari Lwyd," the qualities attributed to the Mari are close to the qualities enjoyed by Taliesin in the *Romance of Taliesin*—he having derived them from Cerridwen through the three drops of Inspiration which fell accidentally on his fingers from her magic potion. It is thus no accident that a number of poems in the corpus actually deal with the saga of this gifted child and inspired bard Gwion/Taliesin.

In his own retelling of the saga, Watkins has defined the ideal poet. In "Taliesin in Gower" (*The Death Bell,* pp. 60-62), Taliesin's power to shift shape, to post across time, and to penetrate and become all essences as told in the original myth, is clearly seen as a metaphor of the poet's mission to translate time into timelessness and draw past into present:

> Yet now my task is to weigh the rocks on the level
>   wings of a bird,
> To relate these undulations of time to a kestrel's
>   motionless poise.

In "Taliesin and the Spring of Vision" (*Cypress and Acacia,* pp. 20-21), the mythic Taliesin is seen as a type of Tiresias, the blind seer whom Odysseus invoked from the shades in his descent into Hades. Taliesin's "vision" in this poem is achieved not by sight but by touch as he gropes for the spring of vision under the rock in the darkness of the cave, symbol for the secret darkness in which light and love reside while awaiting regeneration: the vase or urn which contains the "hidden music at rest", waiting to break out into the music of life, and black repository of the pure white stuff waiting to break out into the light and the colours of life.

> Taliesin took refuge under the unfledged rock.
> He could not see in the cave, but groped with his hand,
> And the rock he touched was the socket of all men's eyes,
> And he touched the spring of vision.

The vital spot is also defined in the poem as "the pin of pivotal space," which reminds us of the pin and pivot in the "Ballad of the Mari Lwyd." When he touched it, Taliesin "saw/One sand-grain balance the ages' cumulus cloud," reminding us of "the covenant caught in a leaf" in "Woodpecker and Lyre-Bird" *(The Death Bell,* p. 48), and of Blake's famous lines in "Auguries of Innocence":

> To see a World in a Grain of Sand
> And a Heaven in a Wild Flower,
> Hold Infinity in the palm of your hand
> And Eternity in an hour.

How is this function of the bard made possible? How is the miracle achieved? Watkins answers in Taliesin's voice that only love redeems time and brings everything together, whether the love between individuals, or the love that is the work of art:

> Earth's shadow hung. Taliesin said: 'The penumbra
>   of history is terrible.
> Life changes, breaks, scatters. There is no sheet-anchor.
> Time reigns; yet the kingdom of love is every moment,
> Whose citizens do not age in each other's eyes.
> In a time of darkness the pattern of life is restored
> By men who make all transience seem an illusion
> Through inward acts, acts corresponding to music.
> Their works of love leave words that do not end in the
>   heart.'

And finally, lest we take the myth too literally, we are reminded that even with his epiphanies, his second sight and his sixth sense, the poet is still but a man, his gifts limited by his humanness. The last note sounded is therefore one of Christian humility:

> Taliesin answered: 'I have encountered the irreducible
>   diamond
> In the rock. Yet now it is over. Omniscience is not
>   for man.
> Christen me, therefore, that my acts in the dark may be
>   just,
> And adapt my partial vision to the limitations of time.'

BIBLIOGRAPHY

Baird, James. *Ishmael*. Baltimore, 1956.

Bayley, Harold. *The Lost Language of Symbolism*. 2 vols. New York, 1958.

Benwell, Gwen, and Arthur Waugh. *Sea Enchantress*. London, 1961.

Berry, Ron. "Vernon Watkins' 43rd Year of Poetry Making." *The Swansea Voice*, April 15, 1960, p. 3.

Blake, William. *The Complete Writings of William Blake*, ed. Sir Geoffrey Keynes. Oxford, 1966.

Bolton, Eileen M. "The Prisoner Gwair." *The Anglo-Welsh Review*, XV, No. 36 (Summer, 1966), 12-13.

Breuil, Henri, and Raymond Lantier. *Les Hommes de la Pierre Ancienne*. Paris 1959.

Chadwick, Nora Kershaw. *The Druids*. Cardiff, 1966.

Cirlot, Juan Eduardo. *A Dictionary of Symbols*, trans. Jack Sage. New York, 1962.

Cohen, John Michael. *Robert Graves*. New York, 1965.

Crampton, Patrick. *Stonehenge of the Kings*. New York, 1968.

Davidson, H. R. Ellis. *Gods and Myths of Northern Europe*. Baltimore, 1968.

Davies, Eryl, Elizabeth M. Jones, Neville Masterman, and Ceri Richards. "Four Tributes," *The Anglo-Welsh Review*, XVII, No. 39 (Summer, 1968), 7-17.

Davies, Jonathan Ceredig, *Folklore of West and Mid-Wales*. Aberystwyth, 1911.

Dillon, Myles, and Nora Kershaw Chadwick. *The Celtic Realms*. New York, 1967.

Eliade, Mircea. *The Forge and the Crucible*, trans. Stephen Corrin. London, 1962.

——. *Rites and Symbols of Initiation*, trans. Willard R. Trask, New York 1958.

Encyclopaedia of Religion and Ethics, ed. James Hastings. 13 vols. Edinburgh, 1908-1926.

Evans-Wentz, Walter Yeeling. *The Fairy Faith in Celtic Countries*. New York, 1966.

Frazer, Sir James George. *Adonis, Attis, Osiris: Studies in the History of Oriental Religion*. 2 vols. Part IV of *The Golden Bough: A Study in Magic and Religion*. 12 vols. 3rd Edition. London, 1927.

——. *Spirits of the Corn and of the Wild*. 2 vols. Part V of *The Golden Bough: A Study in Magic and Religion*. 12 vols. 3rd Edition. London, 1925.

Frye, Northrop. *Fearful Symmetry: A Study of William Blake.* Princeton, 1947.

Gilbert, Alan H. *Literary Criticism: Plato to Dryden.* Detroit, 1962.

Graves, Robert. *The White Goddess.* New York, 1966.

Griffiths, Margaret Enid. *Early Vaticination in Welsh with English Parallels.* Cardiff, 1937.

Hando, Frederick James. *Journeys in Gwent.* Newport, Mon., 1951

———. *The Pleasant Land of Gwent.* Newport, Mon., 1944.

Harding, Mary Esther. *Woman's Mysteries.* New York, 1955.

Hays, H. R. *In the Beginnings.* New York, 1963.

Henderson, Joseph L., and Maud Oakes. *The Wisdom of the Serpent: The Myths of Death, Rebirth and Resurrection.* New York, 1963.

Hirst, Desiree. *Hidden Riches.* London, 1964.

Houlder, C., and W. H. Manning. *South Wales: Regional Archaeologies Series.* New York, 1966.

Howey, M. Oldfield. *The Horse in Magic Myth.* New York, 1958.

Jackson, Kenneth Hurlstone. *The International Popular Tale and Early Welsh Tradition.* Cardiff, 1961.

James, Edwin Oliver. *The Cult of the Mother-Goddess: An Archeological and Documentary Study.* London, 1959.

Jobes, Gertrude, and James Jobes. *Outer Space.* New York, 1964.

Jones, Thomas Gwynn. *Welsh Folklore and Folk-Custom.* London, 1930.

Kendrick, Sir Thomas Downing. *The Druids: A study in Keltic Prehistory.* New York, 1966.

Lavater, Lewes. *Of Ghostes and Spirites Walking by Nyght,* 1572, ed. J. Dover Wilson and Mary Yardley. Oxford, 1929.

La Braz, Anatole. *La Legende de la Mort chez lez Bretons Armoricains.* Paris, 1902.

Loomis, Roger Sherman. *Wales and the Arthurian Legend.* Cardiff, 1956.

The Mabinogion, trans. Lady Charlotte Guest. London, 1910.

The Mabinogion, trans. Gwyn Jones and Thomas Jones. London, 1949.

MacBain, Alexander. *Celtic Mythology and Religion.* Stirling, 1917.

MacCulloch, John Arnott. *Volume III: Celtic* of *The Mythology of All Races,* ed. Louis Herbert Gray. London, 1964.

———. *The Religion of the Ancient Celts.* Edinburgh, 1911.

Malory, Sir Thomas. *Le Morte D'Arthur.* London, 1923.

Mathews, Shailer, and Gerald Birney Smith. *A Dictionary of Religion and Ethics.* New York, 1923.

Mathias, Roland, "A Note on Some Recent Poems by Vernon Watkins." *Dock Leaves,* I, No. 3 (1950), 38-49.

McCormick, Jane. "Vernon Watkins: A Bibliography." *West Coast Review,* IV, No. 1 (1968), 42-48.

Melville, Herman, *Moby-Dick.* New York, 1959.

"Memorial Service Tributes to Poet Vernon Watkins." *The Swansea Evening Post,* March 11, 1968, p. 2.

159

Morton, Henry Canova Vollam. *In Search of Wales*. London, 1941.

Murray, Alexander Stuart. *Manual of Mythology*. New York, 1891.

Orr, Peter, ed. *The Poet Speaks*. London, 1966.

Osgood, Charles Grosvenor, trans. *Boccaccio on Poetry—Being the Preface and the Fourteenth and Fifteenth Books of Boccaccio's Genealogia Deorum Gentilium*. New York, 1956.

Owen, Aidan Lloyd. *The Fabulous Druids: A Survey of Three Centuries of English Literature on the Druids*. Oxford, 1962.

Parry, Thomas. *A History of Welsh Literature,* trans. H. Idris Bell. Oxford, 1962.

Paton, Lewis Bayles. *Spiritism and the Cult of the Dead in Antiquity*. New York, 1921.

Paton, Lucy Allen. *Studies in the Fairy Mythology of Arthurian Romance*. New York, 1960.

Percival, Milton Oswin. *A Reading of Moby-Dick*. Chicago, 1950.

Piehler, Hermann Augustine. *Wales for Everyman*. London, 1955.

Pigott, Stuart. *The Druids*. London, 1968.

"The Poet Who Was Al at Lloyds." *The Swansea Evening Post,* October 10, 1967, p. 4.

Raine, Kathleen. *Defending Ancient Springs*. London, 1967.

——. "Vernon Watkins: Poet of Tradition." *The Anglo-Welsh Review,* XIV, No. 33 (1964, 21-38).

Rees, Alwyn, and Brinley Rees. *Celtic Heritage: Ancient Tradition in Ireland and Wales*. London, 1961.

Rhys, Sir John. *Celtic Folklore: Welsh and Manx*. 2 vols. Oxford, 1901. .

Lectures on the Origin and Growth of Religion—The Hibbert Lectures 1886. London, 1898.

Rolleston, Thomas William Hazen. *Myths and Legends: The Celtic Race*. Boston, n.d.

Ross, Anne. *Pagan Celtic Britain*. London, 1967.

The Sacred Books of the East, ed. F. Max Muller. Vol. XVIV. New York, 1897-1901.

Senior, John. *The Way Down and Out: The Occult in Symbolist Literature*. New York, 1959.

Shepard, Odell. *The Lore of the Unicorn*. New York, 1967.

Skene, William Forbes. *The Four Ancient Books of Wales*. 2 vols. Edinburgh, 1868.

Thomas, Dylan. *Letters to Vernon Watkins,* ed. Vernon Phillips Watkins. London, 1957.

Trevelyan, Marie. *Folk-Lore and Folk-Stories of Wales*. London, 1909.

"Tributes to the Poet." *The Swansea Evening Post,* October 9, 1967, p. 3.

Trioedd Ynys Prydein: The Welsh Triads, ed. and trans. Rachel Bromwich. Cardiff, 1961.

Von Cles-Reden, Sibylle. *The Realm of the Great Goddess*. Englewood Cliffs, New Jersey, 1962.

Watkins, Vernon Phillips. *Affinities*. London, 1962.
——. *Ballad of the Mari Lwyd and Other Poems*. London, 1947.
——. *Cypress and Acacia*. London, 1959.
——. *Fidelities*. London, 1968.
——. *Selected Poems*. Norfolk, 1948.
——. *Selected Poems*. New York, 1967.
——. *The Death Bell*. London, 1954.
——. *The Lady with the Unicorn*. London, 1948.
——. *The Lamp and the Veil*. London, 1945.
——. *Uncollected Poems*. London, 1969.
——. "First Choice." *Poetry Book Society Bulletin,* I (May, 1954), 1.
——. "New Year, 1965," *The Listener,* January 7, 1965, pp. 22-23.
——. "Radio—In Defence of Sound." *Time and Tide,* December 13, 1968, p. 1526.
——. "The Joy of Creation." *"The Listener,* April 30, 1964, p. 721.
——. "The Need of the Artist." *The Listener,* November 8, 1962, p. 756.
Williams, Gwyn. *An Introduction to Welsh Poetry: From the Beginnings to the Sixteenth Century*. London, 1953.
Williams, Sir Ifor. *Lectures on Early Welsh Poetry*. Dublin, 1944.
Williams, Stewart. *Glamorgan Historian: Volume Three*. Cowbridge, Glam., 1966.
Yeats, William Butler. *The Collected Poems of W. B. Yeats*. New York, 1965.
Zehren, Erich. *The Crescent and the Bull: A Survey of Archeology in the East*. trans. James Cleugh. New York, 1962.